Success
ENGINEERING

Phil Gosling

Success ENGINEERING

The incredible real-life science
behind the Science of Success,
and how to make it work for you

Phil Gosling

Quantity discounts are available on bulk orders.
Contact sales@TAGPublishers.com for more information.

TAG Publishing, LLC
2618 S. Lipscomb
Amarillo, TX 79109
www.TAGPublishers.com

Office (806) 373-0114
Fax (806) 373-4004
info@TAGPublishers.com

ISBN: 978-1-59930-387-1

Cover: Lloyd Arbour, www.tablloyd.com
Text: Eric Choi

First Edition

In the next ten minutes you will perform your first miracle. In half an hour you will see how making all the money you want starts with understanding how you can be in two places at the same time. You will play smoke rings with clouds and drive to very strange places in your automobile.

You will suddenly understand that the world that you were taught at school no longer exists, if it ever did.

You are about to step into a real world that isn't real, see things few others see and wouldn't understand if they did, attract your true love like a rocket, and generally be the brainy one at parties. You'll also drive away in the nicest car.

You will see how everything in your life is engineered, and how you can change the design at will.

You're going to go to the furthest reaches of the galaxy and then select reverse and go down to the lower-level parking facility where you can choose your new life from 16 dimensions or more.

If, like the Queen in *Alice in Wonderland*, you'd like to believe in six impossible things before breakfast each day, then this is day one.

And if you don't understand any of this, then you're in very good company, because some of the most talented, qualified, and world-famous scientists, doctors, and physicists don't understand either.

They just know it works.

Dedicated to the memory of Alan Turing (1912–1954), who probably saved a million lives, yet was driven to an early grave by those he saved.

Endorsements

Mind stretching and refreshingly simple. Phil uses science to explain how and why you can achieve your greatest dreams... a must read.

– Andrew Matthews, million-copy bestselling author of *Follow Your Heart* (www.seashell.com.au)

In *Success Engineering,* Phil shows us how our own personalities not only influence our experience with others, but also everything else around us. The idea that the mind influences things as well as ourselves has been alluded to for centuries. In this bold book, Phil reveals that what we think about causes things to happen in the most amazing of ways, and gives us a blueprint for change.

– Dr Darryl Cross, Fellow of Australian Psychological Society (www.drdarryl.com)

Fascinating... clever, entertaining, and mind-blowing. One minute Phil takes you hunting for car parking spaces and the next you're on Pluto, watching the Sun from nearly three million miles away. Just the right amount of "science" to draw me in. If you have a success library (and if not, why not?), then this book needs to be in it.

– Dr James "Tad" Geiger, the oilMD and author of *The Sweet Smell of Success: Health and Wealth Secrets* (http://thesweetsmellofsuccessbook.com)

There is no doubt in my mind that people have a great capacity to engineer the life they want. In his book, *Success Engineering*, Phil Gosling takes readers on a fascinating journey about how we can each use the lens of science and engineering to greatly improve our capacity to achieve the results we want. It is truly a worthy addition to anyone's library on the science of success.

– Di Worrall, author of *A Climate for Change*
(www.aclimateforchangebook.com)

Contents

Foreword

It has been my privilege to have witnessed miracles. It has been my joy to see many people, some from hugely disadvantaged backgrounds, build new lives filled with hope and prosperity. They have often achieved success in a very short space of time, just by understanding how the laws of attraction work in their lives. I speak often about these laws myself and will continue to do so for as long as I am able.

Phil Gosling also found success by adopting these universal laws, but he wanted to find out more. He wanted to find out why they worked, what processes were involved. His natural curiosity was driven by the desire for explanation, so that he too could help people understand how these laws influence every aspect of their lives.

And what he discovered makes hugely exciting reading. By going deep into those areas of science that most people never see or understand, he has used his gift of being able to unravel complex ideas into simple, often amusing explanations to bring encouragement to those who want to know more or see things from new perspectives.

Some of these discoveries are truly staggering, mind-stretching ideas that do more than make you see the world in a new light. You see a completely new world, filled with contradictions and mysteries, a place where computers perform impossible calculations and objects are in two places at the same time. You see the mechanism of how the simplest decision changes not just your own life but also the lives of thousands of others, and how you can alter your own destiny just by observing it.

But what you finally realise is not how small you are in a vast and unfathomable universe, but how great you are and how much control you really do have over your own life. You will see yourself for the great miracle you are and finally discover how you too can perform miracles in your own life. This is not a book about what; it is about why – why things happen, why the laws work for everyone, not just a chosen few. It is the science behind the words, and the science is truly astonishing.

– Paul Martinelli, international speaker, teacher, and coach

Acknowledgements

In the summer of '77, a young man with no money or prospects unwittingly used just one of the ideas in this book to accidentally engineer his life, and thus he bumped into a very pretty and petite 17-year-old girl. Thirty years, two dogs, and four children later, she's still with him, still his best friend. She had married a stargazer – someone who looks at distant horizons and sees things others do not. She guards his feet and stops him tripping over things he can't see because he's looking somewhere else.

Two of the children are like her – practical, intelligent, sensible, fiercely loyal to their friends. Two are stargazers also – dolphins of the universe wondering why all the other fish can't see beyond the surface of the water.

If I said to her tomorrow that I was planning to fly to the moon, she'd give me the usual, quizzical look, then get worried when she realized I was serious. But then she'd instantly give me the encouragement I needed, when anyone else would have told me to wake up and get real.

Everything I've done, everything I am, starts and finishes with her.

The original Internet version of *Success Engineering* was published in early 2004 and became an instant best-seller with well over 24,000 downloads sold worldwide, mainly by word-of-mouth. This was before the huge success of movies like *What the Bleep* and *The Secret*. I knew nothing of these films before

I wrote the book, but as soon as I saw them I shouted for joy. This was because I knew that the ideas in this book pushed science "quite a few steps beyond where it wanted to go." In short, I was afraid of ridicule from real scientists – people who have forgotten more about physics than I ever learned. So when I heard serious and highly qualified scientists like Dr John Hagelin, Ph.D. (Harvard), Dr Fred Alan Wolf, Ph.D. (UCLA), and Dr Amit Goswami, Ph.D., talking of exactly the same things, I could not even begin to express the mixture of joy and relief I felt at that time. And still do. Even though I had sold thousands of books and received many emails from buyers telling me how much this book had helped them, the fact that at least three bona fide giants in the world of physics were independently saying exactly what I had been thinking has been a pivotal event for a professional stargazer. And even though they might not know me or understand why, I thank them for their own courage in taking ideas "beyond where others want them to go," and for making me really chuffed, which of course is the main thing.

It didn't end there. Engineering your success goes beyond the conscious into the very seams and fabric of life. Out of the blue I heard of Bob Proctor and now have the huge privilege of having this hard copy version produced by his LifeSuccess organization.

As a writer I thank Jack Canfield for the gentle inspiration of his own life success, and Andrew Matthews, the million-selling Australian author of books like *Follow Your Heart*, for his friendly telephone chats. Stargazers need company.

Finally, and most importantly, I thank you, dear reader, for also being willing to go beyond where most people dare to go. It's quite a journey.

– Phil Gosling. March 2008.

Introduction

I ABSOLUTELY GUARANTEE you are about to change your entire outlook on life, if not your life itself. During the next hour I will be revealing information that is at the very cutting edge of science, in a place so close to magic that it is difficult to tell the difference. Everything you have ever wanted – the car, the home, the income, *the life* – is so close you can reach out and grasp it. This book shows you *how* to grasp it, how to really succeed. It shows you how to engineer your own success.

Some things remain the same: the fact that you are exactly where you are today because of the decisions you made yesterday; the fact that you accidentally pressed the wrong switches. Press the right switches – and everything changes. This book is all about the *right* switches.

I am going to show you a true secret, the *real* nature of how to get anything and everything you want in life by using a special type of goal-setting I term *success engineering*. This book is probably the first to show you *how* it works, *why* it works, and how you can change your entire life around by using it in this new way. To understand how and why it works will require me to take you where few people have gone before. Even the great mystics of old didn't know why these things work, and indeed neither do you *have* to understand, but I firmly believe that if you can try to understand the mechanics of things, then it will make things so much clearer, as well increase your confidence in them. If you know *why* things work, then confidence appears automatically. Knowledge is confidence. With this new knowledge you will be able to attract success with the certainty of a scientific equation. You will attract possessions – cars, houses, and money. You will attract freedom and create happiness where formerly there was only trouble. If you are lonely, you will attract new people into your life – lovers and friends.

But this is about more than just attraction. You and I are about to share a unique journey. You are about to go to places where you will be one of the few to understand the unbelievable power of numbers, how your brain really works, and how state-of-the-art computers are revolutionizing the way we will all live tomorrow. You will discover Sir Isaac Newton, Einstein, quantum mechanics, free parking spaces, and even a dead cat. And by the end you will discover the strangest truth of all . . .

You *attract* nothing – you *create* your desires, your things, your world out of thin air . . . You *engineer* your future. And I'm going to prove it.

Chapter One
Seeing the Unseen

HI. MY NAME is Phil Gosling. I am a rare event – a nuclear scientist turned entrepreneur, a history that gave me a rather analytical look at things. I have been investigating, studying, and researching another science, the "science of success," for over 25 years. During the past 15 of those years I have personally spoken to or communicated with over 10,000 people. All of these people had the same dreams – financial freedom, time to enjoy things, nice cars. In many cases they also had personal problems, the most common being loneliness in the sense that they were looking for romance.

And for many years I, too, was exactly in that same boat: below average income, on my own, 10- or 15-year-old cars – even a vacation in a tent was a luxury. I have *slept* in my car during vacations – and I mean a car, not a Winnebago. Parking was free. Campsites cost money. Learning physics was not exactly a job ticket.

I have known what it's like to be lonely, poor, unemployed, and desperate, so when I first discovered the principles of goal-setting (starting with Joe Karbo's *The Lazy Man's Way to Riches*) I was smitten. How obvious! What simplicity!

So, over many years, I tried *this* method and *that* system, always knowing in my heart of hearts that the experts and psychologists were absolutely right. Indeed, I was *so* convinced that I carried on believing in goal-setting, reading, and studying everything I could find on the subject regardless of a nagging doubt in my mind. The doubt was that *despite doing these things, my goals were not really happening*. Furthermore, it didn't take a genius to see that most people in the country, particularly those who had also studied books on goal-setting, hadn't achieved very much either. Why did it seem to work for the happy few, while I and most others screwed up?

Like many, I would have given up were it not for a dogged belief, a kind of inner knowledge that within everything I had read was a hidden truth I had yet to discover. And my great good fortune was that in my early years I had tried a goal-setting technique that worked perfectly, and I did achieve a huge goal in my life that I thought was beyond me. That single success made me keep my faith in goal-setting, but I still couldn't understand why in one case it worked like pure magic, yet after that it gave me more stress than success. It seemed that the more I learned, the less effective I became.

Despite the blindingly obvious fact that most people who had read self-improvement books, attended seminars, or listened to endless audio and video recordings were still not much better off, I persisted. Perhaps it's the scientist in me. I could smell a solution to this problem, and like a bloodhound I refused to let it go.

I rediscovered the answer about 15 years ago. The method was so powerful that with my first ever "correct" goal-setting experience I went from unemployed, no car, two kids, and a mortgage to having a top-of-the-line executive automobile in the driveway, and I bought it with cash – all within about 18 months. My life now is unrecognizable from anything I had before. I have the house I want, the car, everything I need. I don't take vacations in a car anymore; now it's a private villa in Portugal. And I didn't get these things by worshipping money or working 24/7 or not seeing my kids grow up. I decided what I wanted, set the correct goals – and they happened. I engineered them.

But that wasn't good enough. I hadn't spent all those years discovering *what* worked. I wanted to know *why* it worked. I'm a control freak. I admit it. Part of this is the debatable idea that if I know how something works, I can fix it if it goes wrong. Up until a few years ago I (and, I suspect, many of the teachers, experts, and self-improvement gurus as well) simply did not know *how* these things worked. Worse still, those who did try to find out, quite sensibly looked at psychology or management theory or business schools to find the answers.

And find answers they did. Their solutions were sensible, well thought out, logical, and conformed to every commonsense notion of why things happen when you perform certain functions. And to this day, these theories, and many others like them, are held in esteem and are taught in schools and universities, not just in the United States but all over the world. And they make sense; that's what matters. They are *scientific* ideas – measurable, logical, methodical, and un-weird. It doesn't matter if they don't work, as long as they're scientific, measurable, logical, methodical, and above all, un-weird.

But just because a guy in a white coat with letters after his name tells me something, it doesn't mean I am obliged to believe it. Even though the speaker is well educated, knowledgeable, dedicated, and expert, that still doesn't mean a less educated, less knowledgeable guy *has* to take on board everything he says. Just because books, libraries, universities, and experts preach that night equals day doesn't mean it's true. Even the best and most well-meaning people – with all due deference to their dedication, education, and knowledge – can simply get it wrong.

Sometimes you cannot see the thing you are looking for until you move away from it. Sometimes you have to change perspective. Drop a blue object on a blue carpet and you will have to get down to floor level and look sideways before you see it.

Similarly, there is a problem with specialization. A specialist, the joke says, studies more and more about less and less until he eventually knows everything there is to know about nothing at all. There is great advantage in *generalization* – having a working knowledge of many unrelated things. It allows you to see things from different angles and see things others do not. It also creates the kind of guy you want to invite to dinner because he can talk to anybody. Doctors of pathology are very poor party animals. Trust me on this.

Although in my college days I studied what was then called theoretical nuclear physics, I openly admit to not being of the highest caliber, and never earned much doing it. But I do understand most of Stephen Hawking's *Brief History of Time*, so I've kept hanging in there while doing my own thing in the entrepreneurial world. And in the same way that some people instantly see certain truths by bringing two different areas of knowledge together, so I, one day, was happily dawdling though a book concerning quantum computers (Y' know, like you do) when suddenly it all fell into place.

What's quantum mechanics got to do with goal-setting? Everything. Absolutely everything. And in this book I will be revealing ideas and information that have never been published before, conclusions and proofs that will take you with me into a world you have never seen before – a world that will turn yours upside down, back to front, and reveal secrets known only to a few people in the world. Soon, you will be one of the few.

And finally, like the Queen in *Alice in Wonderland*, you *will* believe six impossible things before breakfast.

* * *

> *'T ain't what a man don't know that hurts him: it's what he knows that just ain't so.*

> – Frank "Kin" Hubbard

WE TAKE THINGS for granted. It's only when something dramatic happens that we even realize we have taken something for granted. The reason we take things for granted is that they have become part of our routine, and the object of a routine is that we don't have to think about it.

Our lives are filled with routines. Indeed, your whole life can be just one huge routine in which you start every day at the usual time, go to work in the usual way, have the usual time off, do the usual things in the evening and on weekends, and go on the usual vacations. You drive the usual type of car, live in the usual kind of house, and earn the usual income that has been pre-ordained by your usual position in life.

Routines are essential, medically sound, and often unfortunate.

Routines are essential because without them we'd have to spend most of the day thinking about the next thing we have to do and tie knots in a thousand handkerchiefs to remind us what to do next. Without routines we'd all go crazy.

Routines are a way of maintaining the status quo. Not the popular rock combo, but the state in which everything attempts to stay the same. Indeed, medicine has a name for it: *homeostasis*. Homeostasis is what every cell in your body is trying to achieve. It is the state of equilibrium, that point where everything stays the same; where nothing changes. This is part of your natural programming. Your cells are programmed into thinking, "I am alive; therefore, if things don't change, I will stay that way." Cool thinking really, for a cell.

And because you and I are the sum total of a zillion cells working in harmony, then we too, as people, also suffer from corporal homeostasis. With few exceptions, most members of the human race avoid change and like things to stay as they are: If it ain't broke, don't fix it. And when change comes along we don't like it at all – unless it's *good* change, of course. That's okay.

But routines can still be unfortunate. By definition we don't notice them or think about them. So when your lady or man clears off with someone else, it's possibly because you took her or him for granted and never noticed. Routines keep you where you are, in the same place. But most of all, the big problem with routines is that we are blinded by them. They stop us noticing something very important. They stop us noticing the world we are living in. We take the seasons, the sun rising, the green grass, the trees, the air we breathe, life, and even miracles for granted.

Above all, it stops us seeing that we are living inside a miracle; that we are miracles within a miracle. We shouldn't even be here; *life* is against the laws of physics. And those very few people who see this, and study it, discover a strange truth. Not only are we miracles inside a miracle, but we can change things. We have the power. Not only are we in *The Matrix*, but like Keanu Reeves' Neo, we can control it. You ARE Neo.

God does not play dice with the Universe.

– Albert Einstein

Before I can show you how "success" in all its forms can be conjured by you out of thin air, I have to kick you out of the complacency of routine.

Most people don't see the world for what it is. Indeed, most don't see it at all. Until you see the world for the wonder it is, or yourself for the miracle you are, you won't be able to change either of them.

Life shouldn't happen. It's against the Second Law of Thermodynamics. This law simply says that given a system where no energy comes in from outside (known as a "closed" system), then things will either stay the same or wind down, like a clock that is never touched. Because of this law, the idea of perpetual motion – a machine that runs without any energy input – is impossible.

 If you spread a pack of playing cards over a tray and throw them all into the air, what are the odds of them coming down and landing on the tray as a perfectly formed pack? Almost impossible, you may say. Even smaller is the chance of them coming down as a pack with all the four suits in perfect order. In fact, this statistical thinking is wrong. The odds say nearly zero, but this is more than just statistics. This type of event *is against natural law* because the pack must, according to the Second Law, deteriorate over time (unless you interfere with it). The actual odds are therefore *really* zero.

Only the injection of a large chunk of energy (your time and effort) will put the pack in order. If there is no such "external" supply of energy, then the Second Law tells us the pack *must* fall to the ground even more scattered, or at best as equally disordered as when it was thrown up. It can't rebuild itself, not without help.

So, an explosion in a lumber mill could *never ever* produce a fully formed house. An infinite number of chimps banging out letters on a typewriter for an infinite time will NEVER produce, even by accident, a play by Shakespeare. It is as unlikely as gravity reversing and throwing us all off into space. Statistics must always take second place to a law of nature.

Have you ever seen a volcano throw out a bicycle? The makeup of Earth is largely iron and carbon, which happen to be the two main constituents of steel. Steel is made by adding amounts of carbon and oxygen to boiling iron under great heat and pressure. Air contains 20% oxygen, and water contains nearly as much again. All these are freely available in your friendly neighborhood volcano. To make a bicycle frame requires steel tubing. It is a very simple process.

Question: When did you last see a volcano throw out a fully formed bicycle frame? We have had 4 billion years of volcanoes, and all the ingredients are at hand. In that same time (say the scientists) a microbe grew into a Tyrannosaurus Rex. So T. Rex is okay, but why, in the time involved, aren't we drowning in mountain bikes? The fact is that volcanoes have not only failed to produce a single bike frame, they have yet to provide a single sliver of steel. It's a natural law. So where did T. Rex come from then?

A single protein is more complex than the wiring circuit of a mainframe computer, and a protein is one of the smallest building blocks in the human animal, or any other animal. To assume that one single example of animal life came about through a rave of microbes having a serious party in some volcanic soup is to assume that every wire, brick, and pane of glass in Tokyo, Berlin, or New York was created by accident. Human life starting on this incredible world by chance is statistically impossible AND denies a fundamental law of physics. And yet not only do we have life – but in profusion.

Walk past any park and notice the different types of leaves. Why so many, when one type would do? Why such overabundance when simple grass would do the job admirably? The evidence around us every day says that something or someone or (according to your persuasion) the workings of pure chance, has gone completely over the top: a madness of profusion. We are overwhelmed by overabundance.

We float in heavens of incomprehensible size and beauty. There are more species of insects than we have managed to count in the last 200 years. There are sea creatures so far down in the oceans that they have never seen light, yet they breed and reproduce in harmony with the moon's cycles – a moon they have never seen. Without this harmony the earth would spin out of orbit and freeze in space. No life, chaos everywhere; everything running down. If there was only one living thing on the whole planet – a microbe – it would still have been an impossible creation, against a natural law that has withstood every attempt to dispute it for 100 years, and at statistical odds that no hard-nosed betting man would ever take.

You're a miracle inside a miracle. You *know* this. Deep down you know it. But the routine of life has blinded us all to its beauty.

Primitive cavemen concentrated on survival, yet they found time to create art. Modern life is supposed to be about leisure, but we have no time to stand and stare. What you don't know, and will find hard to believe, is the amount of control over your life, this life, you really have.

Let me prove it. Let me prove to you right now that even at an elementary level, you can change your world . . .

It's not that people push you off course; you wouldn't let that happen. What happens is that people nudge you off-center without you even realizing it. After a few miles you're completely lost.

Chapter Two
Engineering Miracles

The impossible we tackle right away. Miracles take a little longer.

 YOU'LL NEED A nice day filled with big, fluffy clouds that are moving at a gentle pace. Lie down in the sun, chill out. Take some rays.

While you're contemplating the meaning of life, check out the edges of some of those clouds. You're looking for a small wisp of cloud, a tiny one that's broken away from a main cloud. Focus your eyes and your thoughts upon that wisp of vapor. Stare at it and *will* it to go away. *Demand*, with confidence, that it disappear, and it will. Just watch. Bob Proctor, the international speaker, reckons he can turn clouds into smoke rings. I believe him. I do it myself.

As a beginner you have to practice on tiny cloudlets. Eventually, with practice, you will be surprised at how effective this can be on bigger ones. And there you are. You're not changing yourself; you're changing the reality around you. Weird or what? (It's to do with energy, quite a lot of it in fact, but we'll get around to that later.)

Sometimes we forget that we are not just *in* this world, we are *part* of it. We not only have a right to be here but if you believe any or all religious writings, then the world was created for us. We have control. God, whoever and whatever you perceive Him to be, has given us the channel changer.

Unfortunately, this experiment will not impress hard-nosed skeptics who will insist that the clouds were disappearing anyway, but we'll move on.

The blue feather

This one often works well but has to be done properly. Make a note of what the date and day will be exactly one week from now. For the sake of argument let's say it will be Friday, the twelfth of March.

Now take a piece of paper and write: *On or before Friday, 12 March, a blue feather has appeared in my life.*

Blue feathers are quite rare. When was the last time you saw one? Of course it doesn't have to be blue, or even a feather. It can be a pink elephant wearing a polka-dot bikini if you want. Whatever you decide, write it down in the manner I have just described. Now first thing in the morning, immediately on rising, find a quiet place and read out that statement to yourself. If you can't read it out loud, then mouth it as a whisper but move your lips.

The more sound and action you put into it the better. Immediately after reading it, close your eyes and visualize this blue feather (or whatever) appearing in your life. *Feel* confident. Smile as you visualize yourself suddenly noticing a blue feather in the street or seeing one on the floor. Put emotion into it. You will see later that it is the emotion you put into it that makes things happen. Do this twice a day, first thing in the morning and last thing at night, every day for one week. I guarantee that within that week, or on the day you chose, you will have come across some image of what you have visualized. You may see it on a billboard or a TV advertisement, or it may actually have come into your life in your aunt's hat or a photograph. But it will appear, quite magically, almost spookily, in your life.

Skeptics will still argue that this just increased your sensitivity to something that was there all the time but that your mind had filtered out. In some cases that's quite possible, but not in all cases. When little green men float out of a flying saucer that's just landed in Washington, D.C., skeptics will still argue it's a publicity stunt right up to the time the death ray hits them.

You are *not* changing yourself. You have *not* noticed something that was there anyway but you hadn't noticed before. You *created* the feather. You are changing reality. And if you think this is spooky, then you ain't seen nothin' yet!

They paved Paradise – put up a parkin' lot . . .

There is a third experiment that works so well I use it all the time. I find car parking spaces with it in busy towns. Just before I leave, I spend a few moments visualizing where I need to park. I see the street or parking lot full of cars until I arrive, and then a car leaves just in time for me to park my car in its space. I see this in my mind's eye before I start the car, feel good about it, and then drive toward my destination with *the confident expectation that my parking place has been pre-booked*. I reckon this works over 90% of the time – far beyond the normal mathematical chance of this occurring by accident. Try it. It works. Appendix C tells you how, but don't go there just yet. We've a few more ideas to cover first.

You're not changing yourself. You're changing something else outside of yourself. In this example it could be argued that *you* changed someone else's day just by thinking about it. Crazy? No. Not at all. This is beyond crazy. This is quantum physics.

Why modern goal-setting rarely works

In a recent *Reader's Digest* article, best-selling author and ex-teacher Philip Pullman put his dark material finger on what's gone horribly wrong with the teaching of English in schools today and also pointed the way to why nearly everything else has been hijacked in a similar fashion.

According to modern thinking by educationalists, particularly those setting examination questions, when a child now reads a piece of set writing, they are "tested for their ability to decode, select, retrieve, deduce, infer, interpret, identify, and comment." So now, for example, when a kid reads a book he or she is expected to:

- List the words used to create an atmosphere.
- Write a 50-word summary of the plot.
- Take a descriptive word from the text and use a thesaurus to find five synonyms and five antonyms.

They have turned reading a book into a chore. *They* have squeezed and analyzed it to death in order to create systems that can be measured and tested. As Philip Pullman says: "They force every response to a piece of writing through a mesh, so it comes out black or white, yes or no, this or that." So it can be tested and measured.

Arguably they did this for all the right reasons at the time. Here again we have teams of well-meaning experts putting scientific ideas into modern practice so that they can quantify and measure a child's progress in the very best interests of the child and their teacher. Again, it is all sensible, logical, universally accepted, and most certainly well meant. But does it work?

Consider a child of the 60s (me) whose English teacher took one book from the library, gave it to me and said, "Read this. Bring it back next week. Tell me if you like it." It was the first real book I had ever read. I was 11 years old and brought up on comic books. I liked it, so Mr. Hudd gave me another book. I liked that one too. No tests, no decoding, selecting, retrieving, deducing, inferring, interpreting, identifying, or damn commenting, just, "Do you like it?"

The net result of developing an enquiring mind is that 50s-60s kids like me were part of a generation who put men on the moon and created the Corvette Stingray and the Jaguar XKE, the Boeing 747 Jumbo and the Concorde. We broke sound barriers, space barriers, race barriers, and generally created a world looked upon with great nostalgia. We were tested, certainly, but when we picked up a book we weren't decoded, selected, retrieved, deduced, inferred, or interpreted, although we were certainly identified. As a result of one teacher just getting me to *enjoy* books, I read a great many of them − because I *liked* them. And through them I found out how things work, and created a life for myself. My teacher's probably dead now. I wonder if he knew how often he changed someone's life without knowing it.

My point is this: In the world of self-improvement, an area of expertise in which America leads the world, many of the teachers, the experts, and the gurus have taken on board *exactly* the same institutionalized thinking currently taking place in schools. This thinking seeks to use the principles of science to analyze things to the Nth degree and break things down, logically and sensibly, into a situation where things can be measured, tabulated, and project-managed. And it all makes sense, every bit of it. And all these guys mean well, and they are doing *good* things. But science has two drawbacks. Sometimes, in taking something apart, you risk killing it. And second, science cannot be used on everything: How can scientifically analyzing works of art produce another Picasso, or a Matisse, or make you enjoy a book?

So, the goal-setting techniques you often read about today are only partially correct. As a result, they only partially work. Indeed, I could go so far as to say that goal-setting has been completely taken over by a new tool *masquerading* as goal-setting. Goal-setting has become project management. And once again it makes perfect sense. The idea of breaking down a process into manageable steps, having a well-defined deadline you can work to, and making each step measurable so you can compare it with your original time estimate and make course corrections is wonderful, perfect, and highly laudable project management. But it's not goal-setting.

And of course, project management is a *management* tool. But managers aren't entrepreneurs. In fact, it doesn't require much research to prove that most entrepreneurs are usually absolutely dreadful managers. What entrepreneurs are really good at is *vision*.

They see what they want with absolute clarity and charge towards the vision with total determination. They make decisions and stick with them. That's goal-setting. Project management is a tool that comes in later, much later, like accounts. The vision, the decision to do it, is first.

Entrepreneurs eventually turn into managers. They atrophy. Once they attain their vision they batten down the hatches and basically leave the running of the show to the bean counters – who manage. Big corporations continue to thrive because they are big enough to carry on under their own momentum. But they never regain the rocket-like success of their early days.

The world of business, education, and politics has been taken over by clever, well-meaning administrators. Here's a comment taken from an article in *The Business* magazine:

"The problem is that business schools, instead of creating leaders, are pumping out hoards of pumped-up administrators. . . . They teach everyone the same orthodoxy. Worse, this orthodoxy can be devastatingly destructive, as it means everyone follows the same strategy as they did in the dot-com boom. . . . The truth is business schools are really just corporate marriage bureaus, matching ambitious administrators with large banks and consulting corporations."

Oops.

Time wounds all heels.

– Jane Ace

So if goal-setting isn't goal-setting anymore, if goal-setting has metamorphosed into project management/administration, what should we do? What can we do?

We need to rediscover the real rules.

At this point, can you please conduct an experiment on yourself by answering, truthfully, a simple question? I have given this question to thousands of people – none of whom got it right. Some *nearly* got it right, but not in all aspects.

It's important you do this, so please get pen and paper NOW before you go on to the next page . . .

Write the answer to this question *as fast as you can*:

What is your number one goal?

Do not leave this page before writing down the answer.

_____

_____

_____

_____

_____

_____

_____

_____

_____

_____

_____

Okay, here's the checklist:

1. Did you start writing right away without having to do any thinking whatsoever? No hesitation, no hemming and hawing? Did you put pen to paper as fast as you would have done had I asked you to write your own name? If the answer is Yes, you stay in the game. If No, you're out of it.

2. Good. What was the *first* word you wrote down? If it was "to" (e.g., "to be financially independent in five years") then you're out of the game. There is only one word – "I." If your statement did NOT start with "I," you're out of the game. If it DID start with "I," you stay in the game.

3. Still in there, huh? Okay, you're in the last 3%, so that's good. Now, what was the *second* word you used? It will probably be a verb, but that doesn't matter. It's the *tense* that matters. Your second word is either future tense ("I will") or present tense ("I have, I own, I drive, I earn"). If your second word was in the *present* tense ("I earn $1 million a year" or "I *drive* a Corvette") then you're still in the game. If it's something in the *future* ("I *will be* . . .") then strike three, you're out.

So at this point, to be in the game, you must have answered the question immediately without hesitation; your first word was "I"; and the whole sentence was in the present tense – as if the goal had already been achieved. If you're still here, then this is very unusual.

4. Did you have any kind of completion date on the goal, such as "by the 31st of December" or "in the next 12 months"? If you did, then strike four and you're off the bench. No dates. Dates are only allowed in certain circumstances, which you will see later.

5. There is a tiny possibility that you are the first person in 10,000 to get this far – or you're kidding yourself, one of the two. Being the generous person I am, I shall assume the former and ask yet another question. Was this goal a financial goal? Was it directed at, say, financial independence? Or expected annual earnings? Did you want to be a millionaire? Oops, you're out. Money isn't a goal. It just looks like a goal. I'll explain that one later. You can have lots of the stuff, don't get me wrong, you just have to think about it a little more deeply.

Well then, how did you do? If you passed all five of these tests, then you did stunningly well. If you didn't get all these right, you *need* to read on. Your future depends on it.

Let me hit you now with just one rule of success engineering, the *true* goal-setting, a rule that seems to flout every piece of advice handed down from the gurus during the last 20 years: *no dates*. Now that's screwed things up, hasn't it? Everything you ever read on goal-setting tells you to put a date on things, even an arbitrary one.

Indeed Brian Tracy, who I personally believe is not human but a benevolent deity sent down from heaven to show us lesser mortals the way to true enlightenment, says that if you do nothing else you should do three things:

1. Set a goal.
2. Make plans for its achievement.
3. Do it while comparing the progress made with your original plan, and make corrections as you go.

And this is perfect. Absolutely nothing wrong with it. Harvard would be proud of him. But there is one problem – what if you haven't got a clue how to get the goal you've set yourself? What if your dream, your goal, was so distant that your education and upbringing never gave you the tools to even consider *how* you could achieve it? Without knowing how to do something, this system will not let you go any further than dreaming.

That's because it's not goal-setting. This is bang-on perfect project management. And it's certainly not success engineering.

The dating game

Goal-setting is not a project management thing.

I know dates make sense; I know having a date on a goal gives you a time frame, and I know it sounds exactly right that you should have a date. But, for reasons you will understand later, it is *not* right *all* the time. You need to think about dates.

A completely arbitrary time frame in a goal ("I will earn a million dollars by

January 6, 2010") can be problematic. Current wisdom says that a date, any date, is important because it gives you a clear time frame, and even if it's arbitrary, things will happen to give you the tools with which to achieve that goal within that time frame.

But a completely arbitrary date to accomplish a task is bad management when you have no idea what steps are involved. Those steps will appear later, and in the meantime the new vision you have of yourself needs time to take shape, like a seed needs time to show above ground before you give it a cane for support. In certain circumstances, as you'll see below, dates are important, indeed vital, but in other cases they are just paying lip-service to project management. Real goal-setting involves a magic that time managers know nothing about. You can't have a system in which proper, logical project management also has to rely on magic, or quantum physics, or tree-hugging in order to work.

One of the few exceptions in which it's okay to put a date on any goal is *if, at the start, you know without question that the goal can be reasonably achieved within that time frame*. So for someone earning 30 grand a year to set a goal of $1 million *by the end of that year* is simply not realistic. Don't get me wrong here; it *is possible* – just not *probable*. Put dates on *reasonably achievable, probable* goals, not improbable ones.

You know this makes sense. If you make a goal of earning a million bucks before December 31, all that happens is you become more depressed and stressed the nearer you get to the date. And if you don't achieve it by that date, you are in the worst of all situations – a failed goal – which makes you even more depressed because this event undermines your entire faith in goal-setting. I'll bet you've been there already. Most people have.

On the other hand, for someone to make a goal of adding 10% to their income in the following year is more than possible. Boring, but possible. You may have to think and stretch things a little, but even if you took a part-time job at Wal-Mart (well, perhaps not, but you know what I mean) then you can see that this goal is achievable. If I offered you a check for $1 million right now based on you adding 10% to your current income by this time next year, could you do it? I'll bet you could. But that's not good either. You need to stretch goals to make them work. You need to push boundaries without subconsciously setting yourself up for a fall.

By the same token, a *certain* goal isn't a goal at all ("By next Sunday I will have fixed that *&!??* leak"). All you have to do here is to add a date and it's a true project management exercise. The same is true for any goal in which you DO have a plan you can work to.

Success engineering – true goal-setting – conjures up the plan. *Then* you can turn the plan into a managed project.

Goals come in four categories:

• *Think-Big* goals. This is a dream that *really* stretches your imagination, because you have no real idea what the time frame is – you don't have a date. You'll see why later. (Example: having that dream home you always wanted.) This is where your goals should be.

• *Reasonably achievable* goals. Not dead certain, they need you to stretch a little. You can put a date on these IF you know it's possible. Use these goals to gain confidence.

• *Emergency* goals. An exception to the date rule. Suppose you are in trouble and absolutely *must* pay your electric utility bill by a certain date, or no power. Even though you may not know *how* it will be done, you must put a due date on this goal: "By January 31, my electric bill is paid in full."[1]

• *Certain* goals. These are anything you know full well can be done; you just haven't got off your butt and done them yet. These aren't really goals. *They are unstarted or unfinished management projects.* Just give them a date and make absolutely sure you complete them in the time allotted. They are only goals in the most general sense and have little value other than to give you self-discipline. And self-discipline is good.

The real reason behind the timing of goals is discussed in Appendix B, but save that for later.

The science of true goal-setting is the science of success engineering. The first step you have to take, and the hardest, is to mentally erase

---

[1] The date is not arbitrary. The date has been set by circumstances and you have to achieve a result within that date. This makes it entirely different from the "think of a goal and then stick a date on it" scenario.

much of what you have read before, because it's not goal-setting. It's an amalgam of project management, time management, wishful thinking, and occasionally original, true, goal-setting, all created by genuinely clever guys who mean well but who have been looking in the wrong box. You need to go back to basics.

When you have done this you will have an open mind. But it's not open enough. I have to break your mind out of its box, so to speak, and show you how much of a miracle it is, and then show you how it empowers everything you do.

Then I will show you *The Matrix*. For here is the truth that I am about to reveal to you in detail: proof of *how* and *why* goal-setting really works, proof that for every goal correctly worded and used, you do NOT necessarily change yourself. For what a goal really does is to *change everything else around you*. If nature is a fantastic timepiece, a huge clockwork mechanism, then success engineering moves the cogs and levers of space apart and restructures the whole system. It changes your world to suit you.

If nature is a computer program, then a correctly worded and carried out goal changes the programming and resets the system – to suit you.

And if you now think I am a deranged and potentially dangerous lunatic then I wouldn't be in the least surprised. But I'm in good company, for in labs in the United States and many others throughout the world, small groups of eminent and brilliant scientists working on the cutting edge of quantum dynamics would completely agree with me. In fact, they'd call me retarded. To them this is old stuff. For what these guys are doing now makes everything you have learned, seen, read, or heard completely obsolete. You are living in the modern equivalent of flat-earth thinking. And 10 or 20 years from now, everyone will simply assume all the things you are about to read are true.

And if you survive this assault on your view of the world, I will show you the real rules, such as the one about dates. But by then you will know *why* they work and *how* they work. And why, unknowingly, you have been using these things all the time without realizing it – for good and bad, but entirely by chance. And you will then use them for good. You will have faith in them. And hopefully you will *do* them – and change your world forever into what you always intended it to be. Your world. The one you deserve.

Chapter Three
The Magic of Numbers

The growth of the human mind is still high adventure, in many ways the greatest adventure on Earth.

– Norman Cousins

I LOVE THIS part. I often quote it at seminars. It is proven, mathematical proof that we are all geniuses, only in different subjects.

The simple fact is that the human mind – your mind – is far more powerful than you can ever imagine. For example, there is evidence that the ancient druids and Egyptian necromancers had knowledge that we cannot even begin to understand. There are suggestions that they had mastered the art of levitation – antigravity. There is evidence that they knew how to melt stone without heat. There is strong evidence that the Great Pyramid was never designed to be just a tomb for a pharaoh or anybody else. Its purpose was older and far more imaginative than a headstone for the headstrong. It was magical.

There is a possibility that electricity was harnessed in the power of simple batteries over three thousand years ago. In India, it is said, there stands a 2,000-year-old iron column that resists rust. We haven't scratched the surface of these ideas but one thing is certain: the human brain is about to be unleashed, and those who look closely at the science surrounding this area will be well rewarded.

So what is this bundle of brain cells we call mind? How powerful is it?

Numbers

In order to understand more about the miracle you are, we need to look at numbers. For most people, numbers have no real significance beyond a few thousand. We can see 10 fingers (okay, I know a thumb isn't a finger) and we can see 100 cars. We can see 30,000 people at a football stadium, but beyond this it is just a number. For the vast majority, numbers like 1 or 2 million are just numbers – they cannot translate these numbers into a picture that has real meaning. We cannot picture a million of anything.

We give numbers names: One, two, up to ten. After twenty they become compound words (twenty-three) until we get to the next real name – hundred. We then compound the hundreds until we get to the next real name –thousand. Then a million. After a million we compound the names into billion or trillion. I regard these as sophisticated compound names because they are all based on the sound of one million, so they don't count as unique names.

Can you think of the unique name of a number larger than a million? (An *aeon* or an *age* don't count, because they aren't specific numbers.) Well, can you? There are two. The first is called a *googol*, and the second is called a *googolplex*, so there's something you can tell the guys over a beer if you want to bore them to death.

These two numbers, indeed most numbers used by mathematicians, are so huge you cannot imagine them or work with them. To make life simple, mathematicians simplify numbers. For example, 100 is written 10^2. The number 2 in this instance is called a power, and to keep it simple it just means that there should be two zeros after the 1.

So 10^2, pronounced "ten squared" or "ten to the power of two," is 1 followed by two zeros = 100. Similarly $10^3 = 1$ followed by 000 = 1,000. In the same way, one million, or 1,000,000, is the number 1 followed by six zeros or 10^6. So far so good.

Now a *googol* is 10^{100}, or 1 followed by one hundred zeros. Well, you must admit that this is one hell of a lot easier to write than:
10,000,000,000,000,000,000,000,000,000,000,000,000,000,
000,000,000,000,000,000,000,000,000,000,000,000,000,000,
000,000,000,000.

Just to test you, a *googolplex* is 10 to the power of a googol. I'll let you work out how many zeros that comes to, and it's quite a lot.

"You're mad."
"Oim in der right place den."

- Braveheart

Of course we are now in cloud-cuckoo-land, so let me tell you what I'm getting at. I'm going to select a specific number, 10^{89}. This is smaller than a googol and it represents the answer to one of the following questions.

1. *Is it the number of people expected to populate the planet by the year 2100?*
2. *Is it the number of carbon atoms in this period . ?*
3. *Is it the number of cells in the average human brain?*
4. *Is it the average number of times a competent politician can evade a simple question?*
5. *Oh, let's go crazy – is it the number of atoms in the whole universe?*

The number 10^{89}, or 1 followed by 89 zeros, is a rough estimate of the number of atoms in the whole visible universe. That's right, the total number of tiny atoms in absolutely everything you've ever seen, and a lot more besides. More atoms than in the Sun, the Moon, and the whole galaxy put together. It is the number of atoms in every galaxy ever seen. To give you an idea of the magnitude of such numbers, 10^{90}, which is just one power greater than 10^{89}, is of course ten times bigger. That is TEN universes put together. And 10^{91} is ten times bigger than 10^{90}, and one hundred times bigger than 10^{89} – that is the number of atoms in *one hundred* universes. Do you see what I mean about big numbers and how few people have any conception of how big they really are?

You need to understand this before you can understand how powerful YOU are.

Your brain

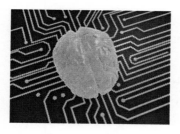

Each cell in your brain is called a neuron and looks like a demented spider whose legs connect with lots of other demented spiders in a gigantic 3-D web of interconnections. Each time you have a thought, the thought is blitzed down one of the spider's legs in the form of a chemical message. That's about how far science has got with regard to the human hat-stand. Even so, this has enabled experts to estimate the sheer power of the supercomputer that is set on your shoulders at this very moment.

You have a brain that weighs about 1.4 kg (3 lbs.). You have approximately 10 trillion brain cells, and each cell connects with 100,000 cells near to it. Every second your brain takes in and stores more information than all the world's computers put together. It receives information from 250,000 temperature sensors, 600,000 touch sensors, and 260,000,000 light receptors distinguishing between over 1,000,000 different shades of color. You can see a candle in the dark 14 miles away.

People liken the brain to supercomputers. This is an insult. A computer is an inanimate, unthinking lump of wood in comparison to your brain. A computer hasn't been invented that can make a two-legged robot walk naturally (although Honda currently has one that walks like an octogenarian waiter on Valium). Your mind goes through more calculations driving a car to work than any computer can possibly handle. Meanwhile your brain goes on thinking about other things while your car is driven almost completely subconsciously, and it even re-routes damaged neuro-pathways at the same time.

In the simple act of crossing a busy street, your brain handles and processes more information than every computer on the planet. It even processes an estimate of another driver's psychological makeup, which means you can tell an idiot when you see one.

Since the early 1950s, psychologists have tried to estimate the power of your brain. They took one of the brain cells and estimated how many connections it could have with other brain cells surrounding it. Effectively it was an estimate of how many "thoughts" can be entertained at one time. This is where our study of numbers comes in.

In those early days an estimate of the brain's "thought capacity" was put at 10^{100} – a googol, no less. Remember what 10^{89} represents? This was fantastic news. Any person's brain – yours, mine, Einstein's – could harness more thinking power than all the matter in the universe. But it didn't end here. By the mid-1960s it was discovered that this estimate was far too low. It hadn't taken all the combinations and permutations into account. As a result, the figure was revised to 10^{500}. Of course we are now definitely over the cuckoo's nest because this number is so huge it has no meaning whatsoever to anyone sane. Unfortunately for us cuckoos, it didn't end here. It gets better.

The most recent estimate of the brain's potential, in terms of the number of connections or "thoughts" it can set up at any one time, is: 1,000,000,000,000,000,000,000,000,000,000,000,000, 000,000,000,000,000,000,000 – now continue this line of 0's for another 9.8 miles. That is $2\times10^{1,000,000}$. Roughly. Give or take a googol or two.

This is not Einstein. *It is you.* This is your potential. *It is, to all reasonable extent, unlimited.* We simply have no idea how to use all of this unbelievable "computing" power. Each and every day you are using a tiny fraction of this just to lead your normal life. Even this amount is greater than any computer ever built, yet it is less than 0.1% of your true potential. Much less.

This information is so unbelievable that science ignores it rather than try to come to terms with it. No amount of thinking can figure out why we have been given so much potential. Even Darwin, who is often misquoted, knew that the human animal was too special to have simply evolved in the manner of butterflies. Animals and humans can adapt to a new situation and only the strongest will survive, but to have been given *an unlimited capacity for greatness doesn't make evolutionary sense.* It is an overabundance of resources. Nature is not usually so overgenerous.

Whether you know it or not, your brain – that is, YOU – has unlimited potential for greatness.

Your three-year-old genie

Your mind has two parts: the *conscious*, which makes judgments and comparisons and is the *awake* part of you (the part you are using now) and the unconscious or *subconscious*, which I can best describe as a three-year-old genie.

Imagine telling a three-year-old kid to boil an egg: "Stand in boiling water for three minutes." The poor kid would try to get his feet in the pan (followed by fifteen lawyers trying to get you in the pan). You have to be very precise with such instructions because a three-year-old doesn't think, he accepts.

In the same way, your subconscious mind doesn't *think*. It's not paid to think – against union rules – that's the conscious mind's job. Thinking is a conscious activity. The subconscious mind just accepts and does. So it needs clear and unequivocal instructions. No ifs or buts. But what does it *do*, this subconscious mind?

Easy question wasn't it? Well, to get the answer, take a degree course in psychology. Three years from now you'll have some idea but you will still be the first to admit that science hasn't even scratched the surface of what the subconscious can do. But here's a quick rundown on what we do know:

- No more than 5% of your brain capacity is conscious, and that's just an educated guess. The rest of your brain is devoted to the part that's supposed to be asleep.

- Most of the motor, chemical, and electrical functions of your body, everything from heartbeat to immune response, are subconscious.

- All memory is subconscious. In a subconscious state you can remember the number of streetlamps you drove past on your way to work.

- There is little doubt that those "creative flashes" like Newton's Law of Gravity or the discovery of the DNA double helix or Einstein's General Theory of Relativity come from the subconscious. A simple study of all the great works in history, all the great inventions, poems, and ideas that have transformed the world, shows that every great notion was the product of some form of subconscious activity:

One evening in 1797 in Somerset, England, Samuel Taylor Coleridge lay asleep after reading about the palace of the Mongol emperor (i.e., the 18th-century equivalent of reading books on quantum computers). He was also out of his head from sniffing opium, a common practice at the time, but we won't go into that. In his sleep he formulated (and then awoke to compose) Kubla Khan, a huge poetic masterpiece, one of the great milestones of English literature. He didn't finish it. A knock on his door by a man from the neighboring village of Porlock disturbed his thinking and the masterpiece was never completed. Arguably, Coleridge didn't create Kubla Khan – he received it. From where?

I could go on but I just want to make two important points:

Expert psychologists like Carl Jung, or psychic phenomenon experts like Dr Lyall Watson, all refer to and accept the idea of a "collective unconsciousness." This is a mind beyond yourself. It's as if the creative thinking of all human beings in the past hovers in the air invisibly by itself. My way of describing this is to consider that somewhere out there in the great unknown is an "idea transmitter," and your mind is not a creator of ideas but an idea *receiver*, like a radio.

This opens up whole new horizons. For example, it means that creative people aren't so much creative, just more tuned in to ideas that settle in their minds from the great unknown. What a brilliant thought! It means that *you don't have to worry anymore about your mental capacity to come up with idea*s. Your mental capacity has nothing to do with it. The ideas are out there somewhere; all you are going to do is draw them towards you. You don't need to invent a fly to catch one. All you have to do is to put up mental flypaper – just tune your brain in to the right channel.

And the second notion is that if all this is true, then there *must* be a connection between your mind and the world outside of yourself – a mental Internet connection with the universe. The 95% of your brain, the subconscious, which we currently think is just sitting there waiting for evolution, is in fact the communications center. It's your connection to the Matrix.

Most of your brain, your subconscious, is a three-year-old genie. Your conscious mind is there to deal with the day, make decisions, and decide your future. It is also the processing unit for your subconscious. It is there to give your subconscious *precise instructions* a three-year-old can understand. These instructions will be simple, logical, and definite. Your subconscious mind uses less than 0.5% of its own capacity to work your bodily functions, drive the car, construct silly robots, etcetera, and uses the remaining 99.5% to turn your "instructions" into a new reality. It's changing the rules to suit you. It's reprogramming the Matrix.

HEY, stay with me here! This isn't even the weird stuff. This is normal. Virtually everything I've said so far is common psychology. The only thing I've suggested that's new is the connection between the subconscious mind and the rest of the universe. And that makes perfect sense.

You see, current thinking says that the world out there is *real*, that it's the same world for everyone, that it's the only world we have, and that we can only change anything in it by picking things up and moving them around.

But it's not. Nor is it flat. As you will soon find out, the world is *not* real; it's different for everyone; it's only one of many parallel universes and has at least 11 dimensions; not only can you change *your version* of the world just by thinking about it, but you're doing it already – every minute of every day. Right now, in fact.

And don't think this is just me rambling on like a deranged fruitcake. This has nothing whatsoever to do with me. This is current scientific thinking. Indeed, the next breed of computers being worked on uses principles that, and I quote,

"... flatly contradict our common sense ideas ... a world where computers work without being turned on; objects found without looking for them ... computers doing their calculations in other universes." - Michael Crichton, 1999.

Trust me, weird is the new normal.

Chapter Four
The Weird Stuff

Decisions, decisions . . .

YOU ARE READING this today because of a Mr. Derek Collinson. In 1969 the corporation Derek worked for *decided* to relocate 200 miles away. He was offered either a severance package or help with relocation. He *decided* to leave the business and stay in his home town. As a result of that *decision* his ten-year-old daughter stayed and bumped into me seven years later. As a result, I *decided* to marry the young lady and *decided* to stop being a bum and carve a life out for us. As a result, I became successful and *decided* to write this book, which you, gracious and intellectual reader, have *decided* to read. Life is full of decisions, and that is why a decision made by my father-in-law changed not only his life, but *everyone else's life connected to that process in the least way.* This includes you.

This isn't weird of course. This is normal. The next bit's weird . . .

At the very moment that Derek made that decision, another Derek made the *opposite* decision, moved and created a whole new life in a different place; a place in which his daughter met someone else, I remained a bum, and everything changed. This took place in a parallel universe in which the *opposite* decision was acted out. Derek, at the time of making his decision, "split" into two and the two Dereks' actions were acted out in real time but in two different universes, each one based on the possible outcome of the decision he made.

"Okay," I hear you say. "I suspect, Phil, that you may be sniffing illegal substances, but in principle you could be right. The film *Sliding Doors* was about exactly that sort of thing and it's an interesting intellectual argument."

"Ah," say I in response. "But if that's true, then *every* decision that Derek, I, you, the president of the United States of America, or anyone else makes every second of every day results in multiple universes being created in which all the opposite decisions are carried out. And this would mean that at this very moment, we are living in but one of an unimaginable number of universes, a number growing all the time with every new decision made."

"Yeah, okay." I hear you say. "So?"

So what if I put a cat amongst the pigeons and say that not only does this happen, but those different universes communicate with each other? Let me introduce you now to some mind-blowing science. Your success depends on it.

An even briefer history of time

Newton discovered gravity and figured out some equations that allow us to predict what happens when we throw a stone, or an

 artillery shell, or a space shuttle into the sky. They show us why our feet stay on the ground, how Apollo 13 got back home, and why planes fly, and everything was all hunky-dory until Albert Einstein came along.

Big Al said Newton's laws work just fine on medium-sized stuff like humans or planets, but when it gets very big – star-sized, for example – then the speed of light messes things up big time. And he devised new rules like his General Theory of Relativity, which is all very interesting and has absolutely nothing to do with goal-setting.

Einstein set a ball rolling because he poked the sacred cow of physics and proved that Newton's immoveable laws were just "good approximations" and when things got very small – atom-sized – then Newton's stuff didn't work at all. So lots of very clever people came up with quantum theory and a whole new set of rules. Weird rules.

And here's a strange thing. To date every prediction based on these rules has worked out 100%. *Indeed, they are currently the most accurate laws ever discovered.* No prediction has ever failed, not one. And these rules are based on a worldview that is not the view most people hold. It's based on a worldview in which there is no certainty, only probability: *a world which changes continuously according to decisions that are made and not made.* Like Derek. Or like you and me when we decide where we're going to park the damn car.

Putting Schrödinger's Cat amongst the pigeons

The Nobel Prize-winning physicist Erwin Schrödinger posed this conundrum to his students in order for them to see the real world more clearly:

Suppose we place a cat in a sealed box. In addition to the cat we place in the box a delicate glass bottle, a vial, of deadly cyanide. If the cat steps on the vial, it breaks, and the cat shuffles off its mortal coil and becomes an ex-cat.

Assuming we cannot see or hear anything inside the box, when the lid closes, is the cat dead or alive? This being *science*, you cannot choose, "Don't know." This is what teenagers say and translated it means, "I cannot be bothered to think about it" or "My brain hurts." In science you cannot sit on fences. It's when you jump one side or the other that progress is made.

So what's the answer? Dead? Alive? What?

The answer is that the cat is both dead *and* alive. In the world of quantum mechanics, when you closed the lid, the cat entered two universes based on whether it stood on the vial or not. And of course, when you lift the lid, you enter one universe or the other. Time travel in a box, you might say. Scientists don't talk openly about universes because such talk scares the straights, so they call it *probability states* and lots more complicated terminology. But don't be fooled. They're universe-jumping.

So, what we've seen so far is that *perhaps*, in theory, we should have a different view of the universe. It's no longer one universe, but many, each based on decisions – on probabilities. Your universe may be the same as mine but with only one thing changed, or lots of things. And these universes can be accessed not by H. G. Wells' time machine, nor even by a box with a cat in it, but by simply making a decision. But let's add another dimension: Suppose that some of these universes interact with each other.

If this is true, the implications are staggering; absolutely mind-blowing. Ghosts could be dead people in one universe appearing in another universe in which they didn't die. Believers and atheists would both be right. Buddhists would be reincarnated and Christians would meet Christ. Heaven or hell could just be parallel, invisible universes so close to you that you could reach out and touch them – and who's to say you can't? In this brave new world Scottie really would beam up to the *Enterprise* because he'd simply change universes to the one in which Scottie #2 had stayed on the *Enterprise* in the first place. In this strange new world you become what you *believe*, simply because you believe it.

Indeed, jumping universes is the only logical answer to a question concerning my lovely lady of many years of marriage, and every guy reading this will recognize the problem. At least once every day I will look for something, not find it, and ask her where this thing is. It may be a jar of coffee or a cookie packet or something. Inevitably she will say, "Top shelf, left hand side, behind the sugar." I will now *not* find it, despite stripping the shelf of every condiment, packet, or jar known to mankind. I will place everything back again, in the full and certain knowledge that it isn't there. Then she will ignore my protests, walk up to the same shelf (usually while reading a magazine), pick the thing off the shelf without looking, and give it to me. She will then give me a condescending smile which translates into "Me, Jane. You, Eejjitt."

She – and, as far as I can tell, every female of any age anywhere on the planet – can do this all the time, and the answer is blindingly obvious. Girls live in a different %@~#`!! universe, and my cookie packet's in it! They're not just from Venus; they live in a different world and can jump universes without even thinking about it.

As far as I'm concerned this should be sufficient proof to any blue-blooded male that quantum mechanics is alive and well and living in your kitchen, but I suppose I'll have to add some proper stuff for the "Of course the Earth's flat, look out of the damn window will ya!" brigade.

Computers aren't scary.
It's programmers who are scary!

Do you know what a quantum computer is?

An ordinary computer is very quick. Indeed that is its only function, to do long-winded things very quickly. And for most things a modern computer is almost instantaneous. But there is still a fraction of time between my pressing a key and the letter appearing on screen. Normally this doesn't affect us, but when it comes to serious computations, computers have their failings.

For example, if I ask a computer to work out the square root of 9, it may start with 8, square it, and see if 8x8 makes 9. If it doesn't, it moves to number 7 and does the same thing. It will do this with all the numbers in sequence until it gets to 3 and discovers that 3x3 is 9 and the problem is solved. For small numbers this is nothing for a computer; it's only six calculations, but when it comes to big numbers (and you know how big some numbers can be) then this process can take a long time – years in fact.

If you want an example, look at computer encryption. If you bought this book over the Internet, your details were kept secret from snoopers because the entire transaction was encrypted (turned into code that others would take a long time to unlock). Indeed for security, private information in my own computer is kept on a "virtual encrypted disk," so even if the computer were stolen it would need the efforts of a major Western government to break into it. That's because even computers need time to do things. That's why scientists are working on creating quantum computers even as you read this.

A quantum computer will work out the square root of nine in a different way. It will simultaneously look at the six computation results on six *different* computers (each computer does only one of the six calculations needed), and each computer is in one of six different universes. The one that gets the right answer spews it out in this one. Effectively it will do all the calculations in the hyperspace world of probability and churn the right answer out here. It will do all the calculations simultaneously and give you an instantaneous answer. No more waiting.

Let's be honest. Isn't this the craziest piece of pure unmitigated balderdash you have ever heard? Multiple, parallel universes *all interacting with each other*. It's the last part that's incredible. I can somehow consider that there are multiple outcomes to every decision and if these outcomes are acted out in other mirror-worlds, then it's feasible, I suppose. But interacting with each other? So I'm supposed to believe that in 1977, my wife in Universe A, interacted with her pa in Universe B (who happened to be in 1969) and told him that moving 200 miles away was not a good idea because the love of her life was only 3 miles away in Universe A, which he would be in if he decided to stay . . . ?

This would be getting seriously psychotic were it not for one inalienable fact. Even Newton knew all this was true. Indeed it was he who proved it nearly 250 years ago. They're still doing it today. If you're interested, here lies just one proof.

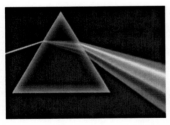

Newton discovered that if you directed a beam of sunlight at a board having two parallel, vertical slits in it, the two mini-beams of light that come out the other side interfere with each other just like water-waves from two stones thrown into a pond interfere with each other. As the crest of one wave matches up with the trough of another, they cancel themselves out. Where crest hits crest, the wave doubles in size. With light, this produces a telltale alternating light and dark pattern on a screen placed beyond the two slits. The fact that light does this "proved" that light moves in waves.

Well, two hundred years ago they hadn't discovered quantum physics, in which light moves as *wave-particles* called photons. So for many years it was generally believed that light acted as both waves *and* particles depending on the circumstances, and two photon "particles" will interact, just like waves. So, photons going through *one* of the two slits in the board will interact with photons coming through the *other* slit in a wave-like manner. No problem – until the smelly stuff hit the fan . . .

If you shoot one single photon at the board – just one – it can obviously only go through one slit. On passing through the slit it should show up as one brief spark on the screen beyond, like a paintball shot though one of two windows splats the wall beyond it. But it's only recently that we have created instruments sensitive enough to project and record *single* photons. So if we shoot single photons one after the other, never in pairs, then each one should pass through one slit at random and hit the screen on the other side. The effect we should expect is the same as shooting individual shots with a single paintball gun at two open windows. We would have the wall beyond the windows splattered in two distinct groups, one group for one window, one for the other window. But with photons it didn't happen. There were four groups, and more, exactly as you would expect with a wave OR interacting particles. *But the particles couldn't interact because two were never fired at the same time.* So how can a particle or wave react with another particle or wave that isn't there? Or, if you like, how can two paint balls ricochet off each other if only one is flying at a time?

The answer was conclusive. The single photon particles *must have been* interacting with other particles. But what particles? Where were they? It was the *same* particle – but the one that made the "decision" to go through the other window. (There is another, modern example in Appendix A.)

Today the scientific community is split in two. Those who simply don't know (*my brain hurts*) and refuse to believe the one improbable solution, and those who see no other answer than the fact that the photon-particle we shot at one slit in this universe reacted with the *same* particle in Universe B – *the particle that made the opposite decision to go through the other window.* Two universes interacting with each other. One universe we can see, because we're in it, and another we can't see, *but its invisible presence is still interacting with ours.*

What correct goal-setting really does . . .

I know this all sounds weird or even spooky, but it's not. It's science. As natural as green grass. It's just our *understanding* of how the world works that's changed. That's all. Indeed this understanding changes all the time.

In 380 B.C., a philosopher called Eratosthenes worked out that the Earth is round by shoving a stick in the ground and watching its shadow for a year. (Clearly, reality TV had not yet been invented.) But it served to change a previous world view that the earth was flat. It isn't always so easy. When Galileo agreed with Copernicus and dared to suggest the Earth moved around the Sun, not only was he not believed, he was imprisoned for heresy.

Today we have an entirely new vision of the world, and I won't be in the least surprised if this becomes common knowledge in 50 years' time. "*Hey, Joe. How about a few beers in this universe while the girls go shopping in the next?*" Or something like that.

And now you can see how goal-setting really works. It's nothing to do with project or time management or drawing things towards you or animal magnetism or altering your cosmic awareness. It's to do with making *a firm and irrevocable decision* and actually creating a new universe, a new life, in which that decision is carried out. You're not changing yourself. You're changing the world.

This isn't new. You're doing it every day. Starting from the day you were born, you are here today because of the decisions you made or decisions made for you each day during your life. And each time, your multi-universe changed according to the decision made.

And by decision I am talking about *real* decisions, not aimless wish lists. Let's look at decision making, because it's important you know what a decision really is.

"Unless you change what you are, you'll always get what you've got."

Chapter Five
Brave New World

I may decide to do today what I should decide to do tomorrow and I may decide to do tomorrow what I should decide to do today . . .

– Old Skipping Rhyme

A DECISION IS a conscious process. Unlike most animals, humans have the ability to consider the future in detail. We can make decisions that affect us *now*, such as which toothpaste to buy, and we can make decisions that are placed on hold for the future, like where to go for next year's vacation.

Both these kinds of decision leave no room for doubt, no room for disbelief. The decision to buy Brand X toothpaste is done and dusted the moment it's in the shopping cart. The decision to go to Disneyland next year is made, and the rest is just detail.

With the first instantly completed decision (for the toothpaste does not require the intervention of any subconscious effort; it was just made, done and dusted), your universe changed to one with Brand X in it. Your decision-making process was unencumbered by thoughts over whether you could or could not afford the toothpaste. There was no doubt, nor consciously recorded belief. It was obvious, which you should read as "belief that is so true that the very act of having to believe you believe is unnecessary."

The vacation decision was also not fraught with questions such as whether you could afford it or not. You just decided that Disneyland was the place to go next year, period. This firm and resolute instruction passed unknowingly into your subconscious mind, and equally unknowingly your subconscious mind took this fixed, unequivocal instruction and started to create a universe in which this will take place. There was no doubt about the decision, no uncertainty, no wavering, and certainly no subliminal belief that you couldn't afford it or not get there.

We tend not to make decisions, *firm* decisions, to go to Disneyland if we expect we cannot afford it. Then it's not a decision – it's a wish, a dream, a nice thought. Firm decisions, *proper* decisions, made without qualification are characterized by *authority and certainty*. The decision is simply *made* – no ifs, no buts, no maybes.

This can also be expressed as having *an absolute belief* in the decision. For the purposes of this book the word *decision* does not mean a wish, or *intent* to try[2] something. It is firm, resolute, obvious, without question. **It is marked by the complete absence of doubt**. When you absolutely believe something, it begins to materialize in the real world according to the strength of that belief. Nothing happens, until you make such a decision.

---

[2] "No try. Either you do, or you do not. There is no 'try.'" -Yoda, *Star Wars*

It's obvious. If we get away for a moment from the multi-universe vision to the scientific equivalent of probability states, it's obvious that until you actually open the box with Schrödinger's cat in it, nothing happens. You don't know the outcome. The opening of the box is a firm decision and that process slam-dunks a probability into a certainty. *Making a firm decision without the slightest area of doubt, a decision made with conviction, is the only thing necessary to change a probability into a certainty.* And when you do this, the cogs and wheels of the universe realign to turn your wish into your truth. Unlike Neo you don't need to train in order to change the Matrix, you just need to believe. You just need to make a decision.

"When you get sad it always seems to rain."
"Lots of people get sad when it rains."
"No baby . . . it rains because you're sad."

– Men in Black II

Brave new world

Your world, or at least your understanding of how it works, has now changed. The notion that you are just you in this fixed world, where in order to change something you had to pick up an object on the Earth's surface and move it somewhere else, has now changed to a new existence.

In this brave new world, the you reading this book is but the you who made all the decisions necessary to reach this point. There are a googol of other "yous" who made other decisions who are now in other universes acting out those decisions. There is a you out there who's a millionaire. There is also a you out there who's a hobo.

The Earth you thought was solid beneath your feet never was. It consists of atoms that push up against the atoms in your footwear. This upward force is electromagnetism, and because it is stronger than the force of gravity, you do not descend into the bowels of the Earth as if you were standing on water. Arguably, if you believed it enough, you could overcome both these forces and the atoms in your body would pass smoothly between the atoms in a wall – and you could walk through walls. Mind the floor though.

The way to change the kind of universe you want to be in, the way to change your future, is to make firm, definite decisions about how you want your universe to be. Doing this creates, invisibly and seamlessly, a new universe in which this new decision of yours is acted out.

Making a decision changes your Matrix. Simple, isn't it?
Ah, no. Actually it isn't. You need to know the rules.

The rules

The first rule of this brave new world is that you cannot change the core program. Again, let's take *The Matrix* as our example[3].

In the movie, the world was a hugely complex series of interlinked computer programs. Everything and everyone in it was a subprogram.

---

[3] Before *The Matrix* came along I tried to explain success engineering in terms of mechanics – the cogs and levers of the universe. In 1993 I started referring to what I called a "reality interface" and the idea that life could be likened to a computer. Thanks to this film, explanations and examples are much easier!

People, cars, trees, and clouds were programs. The combined effect of all this – a harmonious world – is what I call the core program. Individuals in the movie learned the ability to change how they themselves (i.e., the subprogram that is *them*) interacted with the whole or core program. Neo could defy gravity, but he never altered the main parts of the core program. In the movie, the world was still the same, clouds still moved through the sky, the Earth was still beneath his feet, and above all, he could only change himself, not others. He was still *in* that world. He couldn't change the world itself, only his relationship to that world.

Neither can we. Even if, through the correct use of goal-setting, we create a new version of it *for ourselves*, we are still restricted by two things: the degree to which we *believe* the goal we create for ourselves, and the degree to which that goal affects the rest of reality, in particular, other people. We cannot change anything else in the world except our "local" world, and it has to be in harmony with the rest – the big world. World peace is certainly a laudable goal, but I suggest that war is part of the core program, if only because so many more people than you seem to want to engage in it.

In practice, I have noticed that the "big world" issue isn't an issue. The real issue is one of belief, and for most people, generating sufficient belief to change small things, like car parking spaces, is hard enough. Jesus said that with enough belief you could move mountains and cast them into the sea. Moving mountains is a big-world issue that carries this book far beyond where I want it to go. Arguably God is the only one who can alter the core program. For now, why not just change *your* world to one that contains those inanimate things you want but don't currently have. And for the vast majority, that change will need all the belief they can muster, because most people have absolutely no idea what they want.

The biggest problem of all – deciding what you want

The first, and hardest, part of real goal-setting is simply deciding what you want. By that I mean: Is your goal a goal?

Imagine going on vacation. You want to buy an airline ticket. You know exactly where you want to go. You want to go to somewhere with lots of sun, clean beaches, glorious swimming pools, and palm trees. You want to go to "warm and sunny."

Try and buy a ticket to "warm and sunny." You can't. The ticket agent knows exactly what you mean; he probably wants to go there himself, but in reality "warm and sunny" doesn't exist. Unless you tell the agent exactly which location you want to go to and exactly the date you want to go, then you cannot get there. Paradoxically, there are no flights to "warm and sunny" even though most flights go there.

One of the most common goals I have seen people make (those few people who actually make goals) is: "To be financially independent." That is the monetary equivalent of "warm and sunny." It is entirely meaningless, and yet everyone knows what is meant by it.

Your subconscious mind is the equivalent of a mindless ticket agent. It doesn't question, argue, or suggest. If it receives unequivocal, precise instructions, it gets on with it. If there is any "thinking" to do, or if the instruction isn't perfectly precise, it just hangs up. A computer at least gives you a warning: *This program has performed an illegal function and will now shut down; tough.* Your subconscious doesn't. It just does nothing, like an email that's sent but gets lost in the tubes.

Which brings us nicely to rule #2: You have to take each goal back to the lowest common denominator – *you have to be precise.* You have to be certain that your goal is a destination – not a flight.

Money is a flight, not a destination. To have a goal of "financial independence" will not work because this instruction contains no details of exactly what this means. Does it mean $1 million in the bank? $2 million? Does it mean owning several rental properties? What?

I can prove to you that money is not what you want. Suppose I offer to write you a check for $1 million – and repeat it every year. But there is a catch. You will have to live on your own on a desert island. You can have any car or house you like, so long as you pay for it out of the $1 million a year and you have them on the island – on your own. Would you take this?

Some would; most wouldn't. What's the point of cash in the bank? It's what you buy with it that matters. Of course the reason why $1 million in the bank sounds exciting is because:

1. You wouldn't need to work any more.
2. You would know that all your bills and expenses now and in the future are covered.
3. You could up your lifestyle.

The first two are all about security – an inner fear that you won't be able to pay your bills in the future. It can turn into an endless hunt for

the next $1 million or the one after that. I call it buffalo hunting.
My idea of security is to metaphorically live near enough buffalo
so that when I need one to feed my family, I just go and hunt one.
That single buffalo may be all I need to feed and clothe my family
for a year. I can understand those who hunt two buffalo, one for
the current year and another for one year ahead. But most of the
millionaires I have seen and often spoken to are the equivalent of
manic buffalo collectors. They want/need hundreds of buffalo. Does
this make them happier? More secure?

I'm not so sure. These men seem constantly driven. Why do they
need this overabundance? Why can't they just have *enough*? Are
they compensating for something? With a hundred buffalo pelts in
storage, their fears change to protecting those pelts from thieves.
So they lie awake at night worrying. This type of goal can often
produce more problems than it solves, and this desperate pursuit
of riches is very debatable in terms of human happiness. Wealth is
more a state of mind – a *knowing* that money is available to you on
demand, as and when you want it. It's not the need to collect piles
of green paper.

> *People assume that happiness stems from collecting things*
> *outside of yourself, whereas true happiness stems from removing*
> *things from inside of yourself.*
>
> – The Dalai Llama

For example, my notion of financial security is to have a small, highly
profitable business (or businesses) that demands little attention and

will keep me occupied for a few hours a week. The rest of the time it looks after itself. I could do that until I am a ripe old age and not worry about money, or panic every time the stock market takes a tumble. If I become ill, I have the business managed, or take out insurance, or both. What's the big deal?

As for upping your lifestyle, consider why. Is it to impress someone else? I like to run my purchases through a number of filters before I buy. I ask myself – would I buy this if I were the only person on the planet, and who am I trying to impress? Would I buy this if I were completely on my own? I own a classic roadster. Would I have it if no one saw it? (Damn right I would. It's great fun.)

An example of a perfect goal is a car. I know this is a man thing but I have certain limitations with being one.

"I own a nice car" and "I drive a Ferrari" are not good goals because they are not precise enough. "I own a Range Rover V8i in dark blue, with cruise control, ABS brakes, air conditioning, alloy wheels, and a five-speed stick shift" is a perfectly worded goal. It is so precise that you could give this information to Honest Abe's Car Emporium tomorrow and he'd order it right away. You can't buy "a Ferrari."

Words are important too. "I drive a Ferrari" is different from "I own a Ferrari." See the difference? Every goal you decide for yourself must be well thought out and very precise. There are rules to the game. Goal-setting is a process where you give your conscious mind precise, absolute, and firm instructions. These are passed to your subconscious, and provided that there is no room for doubt, the subconscious will power up its $10^{1,000,000}$-watt communication center and suddenly the quantum universe starts to realign in your favor. How fast it does this depends on the strength of your belief, the exact wording of the instructions, and whether you are restructuring your "local" world or trying to be Buzz Lightyear.

Chapter Six
Quantum Goal-Setting

 COMMUNICATIONS ARE VITAL. The most important school subject should be a combination of the English language and "human communication." The reasoning is simple. If you cannot make yourself understood, then you are several goals down before you even start the dramdring frog basket.

Nearly everything you want is either controlled or owned by somebody else. In order to persuade them to give it to you, you need to make yourself understood. Wars have started because messages were misunderstood. (The 1881 Boer War started when a comma was left out of a telegram.)

In the military and aviation they take this so seriously that communications are restricted to fixed phrases. If you're going to communicate anything, it must be crystal clear. That's why goal-setting has rules.

For over 15 years, in conjunction with others, I have been testing goal-setting systems to see which work and which don't, or which are goal-setting and which are glorified project management. I didn't invent these systems; I merely tested which of them work, and which don't. The following axioms make all the difference between success and failure. They are the inviolate rules of success engineering.

1. Goals must be written down.

This is because you must reinforce them by using as many of your senses as possible. In writing them down you are using your eyes and hands. When you repeat them to yourself later, you should, wherever possible, rewrite them or at least repeat them out loud. Even if it is impossible to read out loud you can still whisper and move your lips.

Not only should you write your goals down, but later on you will see that we are going to make a ceremony of it. After all, this is arguably the most important exercise of your whole life. It certainly holds the greatest promise. You should use the best quality paper and the best pen you can get hold of.

2. Goals MUST be written in the first person – "I . . ."

All goals must start with "I." You cannot make a goal for anyone else. Goals are only for you, and they are intensely personal. So, every goal you choose for yourself must be written in the form "I own . . . I have . . . I am . . . I drive . . . I live in . . ."

3. Have at least one psychological goal involving a positive change in your attitude. Word this goal as if it were already true in your life.

Psychological goals, you will remember, are those goals involving mental states such as concentration, courage, or being positive. Basically, they are all different forms of one major psychological goal, and that goal is *strength*. You want to be strong to meet life's challenges.

Now think carefully: You cannot *prepare* to become strong, not mentally. If it is physical strength, then yes, you can prepare by doing physical exercises. But this only works for physical strength. *Psychological* strength cannot be prepared for. You cannot, for example, say, "I will be bold next week." It doesn't happen that way.

You are already strong. You have within you all the strength you will ever need. Consider that you already are a strong person, but your belief mechanism has put a lid on it. The way to release the lid is to accept that today, now, you are already strong and that each day your newly discovered source of strength increases.

All psychological goals should be worded *as if you already possessed* that particular virtue, and its intensity is growing stronger each day.

"I have great strength of character. It increases every day."
"I have absolute belief in myself, made manifest in everything I say and do."

To see your worst enemy – look in a mirror

During the last few years I have been tutoring individuals in special business areas. I have also been in contact over the years with thousands of similar individuals, and I see patterns. Without question, the main reason why these individuals haven't succeeded in some business or other *is entirely down to their attitudes or inner beliefs in themselves*. Notice I said in themselves, not in the business. I have seen thousands of people search for a business opportunity that they think will, by itself, provide 99% of the success they crave while they contribute 1%. The sharp reality is that most success stories are 1% the business, and 99% the person's belief in him or her self.

I have seen innumerable hopefuls spend huge amounts of money in their desperation to start some enterprise that will give them all the hopes and dreams they aspire to. And despite personalized "do this next" instructions, I have seen many people fail and fail again due entirely to a firm inner belief that they "couldn't do it." The trouble is that these people do not know this is going on inside them. They talk constantly of success yet still harbor an invisible, unshakable, and unconscious belief that they cannot do these things, usually inspired by a poor self-image. It works like this.

Suppose, due to financial constraints, a person has always had to buy second-hand cars. If asked to buy a new one, they would look at their finances and decide they could not afford a new car. That seals their future. They are in a loop but cannot see it. They have looked at their current situation and made a decision about their future based on their past results, a decision that has put a ceiling on what they think they can afford. Their self-image remains the same and puts a halt on all progress.

Suppose that same person invests in a business opportunity (assuming it's a good one). Their current situation is that they've never done very well at these things, and therefore they let this "failure" or "I am what I am" mentality dominate their aspirations. As a result they only give the opportunity a half-hearted prod, and if it doesn't produce results in five minutes they give up. This reinforces their current self-image, and the cycle repeats itself.

On the other hand, deciding to buy that new car in spite of the fact they cannot afford it invariably frees the person's mind to search for new ways of paying for it. When they achieve that end, their self-image has been raised to a new level and from now on they buy new cars. This leads to buying better new cars and finding better ways of paying for them, thus creating an upward, positive spiral of success based on new self-images.

I have said to you that a firmly held belief in any goal actually changes your universe to bring it into reality. And so it does, even to your detriment. It's important to comprehend that it's NOT what's in your conscious mind that affects the Matrix; it's what's in your subconscious mind, the one with the USB socket to the universe, that affects your world. Your conscious mind can wish for $1 million all day long but it's only when you subconsciously *expect* it to happen that things start moving.

This happens all the time. You are, today, an exact reflection of what you subconsciously think you are, whether you like it or not. The only difference now is that you can see that you have the power to change it, and remarkably quickly.

Something very strange and unexpected happened when I tried to tutor certain people. Part of the business plan I presented to them included, quite naturally, the powerful goal-setting techniques you are reading here. The reason for repetition and visualization of these goals, and also the extra input from self-improvement and motivational tapes, books, and DVDs, is to overwrite people's subconscious negative belief in themselves. I knew this in-built negative belief (we all have it; it's homeostasis) was strong, but if the quantum universe information in this book is true, that negative belief would have an equal but negative effect on those who focused on the wrong things. It would NOT create the universe they were paying lip service to, the universe they *wanted*, but WOULD create their innermost fears – the things they really *believed*.

So I fully expected a *psychological* backlash when I started to push people. What I didn't expect, oddly, was the *physical* backlash. I expected some to fail simply because of psychological resistance – all those hidden habits and paradigms that held them down. These people simply failed to go forward, or found 10^{89} excuses and reasons for not doing what I told them to do. But what I didn't consider was the possibility that, with my trying to push them *through* this barrier, their own minds (unable to counter my pushing with psychological excuses), would then **create** real *physical* circumstances that would definitely prevent me pushing them beyond their innermost beliefs.

I am not going to frighten you away from any of this by giving you some very spooky and sad examples, but I will give you one story because it's a very powerful example of negative "universe creation."

We'll call him Joe. Joe was involved in a boot camp where I was actively pushing him to create a certain web-related business. He was "certain" he could do it. He was optimistic and enthusiastic. He was not very computer literate but he knew enough of the basics.

If you start a small home-based business you go through stages. First, there's the honeymoon period where it all looks exactly right, just what you had always wanted. Then comes the reality check – you have to think, act, and plan. You suddenly realize it's 99% YOU. This is not taught in schools, so most people start getting a severe dose of the gremlins at this point, which is exactly why they need the support of someone who's done it before. Most people stop near or at this point with excuses: *it's too difficult, I've not enough time,* etcetera.

In reality, it is their in-built belief that they cannot do this thing, that they're not cut out for it. I thought, in my arrogance, that if I stepped in and pushed such people forward (without first resetting their belief structures), they would get over this barrier. Those people who actively and consistently used these goal-setting techniques to change their inner belief systems did make further progress. But what I hadn't expected was what the quantum aspect of goal-setting would do to those who didn't alter their self-image.

Put simply, if someone exists in a universe where he or she thinks they *cannot* do something, then, if pushed beyond this barrier by another person, they will start to psychologically sabotage themselves, for example by being tired, or making all kinds of largely invalid excuses. But if you push some of these people beyond the point where psychological avoidance methods won't be enough, *then the subject will actually alter his/her surrounding universe in order to create physical circumstances that will, without question, stop all progress.* What I'm saying is that a person's inner negative belief can be so strong it creates a *physical* obstacle to making progress.

It started psychologically. Every time Joe had a problem he emailed me. I had 180 emails in three months. I have helped people with computer problems on thousands of occasions but it seemed to me that absolutely everything that Joe did, computer-wise, simply went sour every time. I would send passwords to various people to open files – Joe's didn't work. I would send emails others received but he didn't. I would ask people to look at certain websites. He couldn't get onto them. I have never, in my whole life, seen a situation where every solution only partially worked or failed completely. I just assumed he'd convinced himself that it was all too difficult.

So he came to my house, and I sat at my own computer and showed him how to do something. Then he sat down at the same computer and I showed him what to click – and it didn't work. *He* was actually physically affecting the computer and the Internet. In his universe the Internet didn't work, because he believed it so. It was the only way to stop me pushing him beyond his comfort zone. This was one of my first observations in the power of quantum goal-setting and it was happening to someone completely subconsciously.

The idea of creating a new universe for yourself containing those things you want is made easier to believe by showing you the opposite, that people can actually bring physical disaster upon themselves simply because they believe themselves unlucky. I'm sure you know people like this. They are just doing the same thing: watching what they believe to be true actually come true in their lives. So think lucky! For God's sake, think lucky.

In my opinion, only two types of people ever achieve the success they crave:

- Those who believe they can, deep down. They are *belief*-driven.

- Those who have no choice. They are *fear*-driven.

It's all down to belief in yourself – or fear. The business you choose rarely comes into it, because a business is itself a vehicle, a flight, not a destination. The success stories of the world either were those people who were *absolutely determined* to achieve success, or those who consciously or unconsciously used goal-setting techniques, or those whose backs were against the wall and were forced to go beyond where they wanted to go. They either had a self-image that was a positive, upward-spiraling one, or they blasted through the "terror barrier" of limited self-belief and made progress that way.

So who *didn't* win? People in the comfort zone of JOB (Just Over Broke). Breaking through the self-belief structure, a structure that has been created out of your past experiences, sets up a homeostatic response. In practical terms, homeostasis, which is a medical condition that wants you and everything about you to stay the same, will unleash your personal four horsemen of the apocalypse – fear, doubt, uncertainty, and stress – every time you force change. This is the "terror barrier" you have to go through. For most people in the comfort zone of JOB, it is easier to simply give in and retreat back to the comfort of the mundane than to face the effort of trying to go beyond where they think they can go. This is a huge pity, because in most cases the devil is nothing but smoke and mirrors.

It has been my observation that success tests you first. Your inner resolve is put to the test in order to tease out weaknesses in your desire. It examines whether your decision to be successful was a *decision*, as I define it, or a wish list.

In the millions of rags-to-riches examples of successful people, many are immigrants from countries having no welfare support for their poor. Their desire to become successful came simply from the fear that they must not fail. They dared not fail. Failure = starvation, which was simply not an option. Without question, the bulk of self-made, successful millionaires come from poor, disadvantaged backgrounds. In their cases, the decision to be successful was indeed a decision. To fail was to die. It was this that pushed them through the terror barrier.

When such a person encounters a problem, a hurdle, a blockage on the high road to accomplishment, they make the effort to overcome it. They refuse to give up. They either dare not give up or are absolutely determined not to be beaten. By contrast, when someone who is in a poor but reasonable job and who wants "the better things in life" meets the first hurdle, he/she has a back-out plan. The back-out plan is the fact that they need not go down this road; they have an income already, however bad. Their determination is weak, most often stemming from a pure lack of confidence. This lack of confidence, plus a wish for better things, lures them down the wolf-ridden forest path of "easy money" or business opportunity rip-offs: businesses that promise easy money for no thinking or preset plans. Yet no matter how juicy the business looks, the successful people within it will have applied 99% determination to 1% of the business – any business – not the other way round.

Success simply requires self-belief and determination. Make goals for them.

4. For physical goals you must write down EXACTLY what you want, BUT NOT the date by which it will be achieved – with one exception – the Emergency Goal.

For physical goals, like a new car or house, you must be precise but you must NOT specify a deadline for its achievement. An Emergency Goal, on the other hand, is a critical goal that has a time limit set by circumstances outside your control. For example, you may need to pay an electricity bill before the end of next month or you will be shut off. Or a tax bill before the end of the month or you will get locked up. These goals are always dated ("By March 15 my electric bill is paid in full").

Let me give you an example of a goal I created for myself which was quite hard, but I did a live test specifically to show you how to attain a goal.

In order to get fit but to avoid the back trouble that 15 years of football had produced, I had taken a keen interest in cycling. I did not have a mountain bike at the time, only an old rattletrap, but instead of just going out and buying one I decided to write the following goal, and because I decided it was an Emergency Goal, I dated it:

"By September 15 I own an excellent mountain bike. I obtained this free of charge or cost." (Notice that it's present tense even though the grammar is way off.)

Now that's tricky. Getting a decent bike free of charge. I didn't know enough about bikes, or care enough to be specific as regards color. And by "excellent" I meant one that would do the job. What I *should* have said was "21 gears with cantilever brakes," but anything would have done just for this test. I freely admit that standing under Mount Etna with outspread arms was an option I hadn't considered, but we'll move on.

Over the next few weeks I repeated and visualized this goal and as each day went by nothing happened. I looked in the local paper but of course everything in it had a price tag attached, so it wouldn't count. Now, to be honest, I did include a time factor in this but that's because I know how time factors work, as I shall explain in the appendix. Putting dates on goals can be very tricky and *you need to know what you're doing.* My advice is to not use dates except in specific circumstances such as Emergency Goals. With days to go I thought I'd finally cooked my goose.

I even thought that I could exchange something for a bike, but the opportunity never arose. When the day arrived I thought I had totally failed. Not one single opportunity had arisen for completing this goal.

You see, setting a date is very difficult. First you have to think about how long it will take to complete the goal. Most people have no idea and choose an arbitrary date. A free bike in two weeks I considered to be too short, so I just chose four weeks at random. But the major problem is that by choosing a date, *you set up a potential failure date.* This can produce stress as you get nearer the goal. That's because we are conditioned to think in straight lines. If we are halfway through the goal-setting time limit, we should have half the goal already. Yet nature does not have straight lines.

The last thing you want is to *not* achieve a goal, because it places all your other goals in jeopardy. The fear devil inside you will have a field day —"Forget it," it says to you in the depths of the night. "It's all rubbish. You've no chance." And so it goes on.

The temptation is to compromise. NEVER COMPROMISE, JUST DO IT. JUST DO IT is the best advice on earth.

Oh, you want to know about the bike, don't you? On September 16 my sister-in-law rang me out of the blue to tell me her neighbor had given her an old bike that he didn't use any more, and the tires were flat. Did I want it?

Guess what? It was a 21-gear mountain bike with cantilever brakes. Well used, admittedly, and with a puncture. The repair cost 95 cents, and I didn't actually receive the working bike until one week after the goal deadline had passed. Well, you could say that the goal failed in that I didn't achieve it on *exactly* the set date, and it did cost 95 cents. But then again, one week later I was running around on a 21-gear mountain bike, having spent a few cents on a repair, not on a purchase, so who cares? My universe had changed.

Remember, in all goal-setting you are defining the center as your target. Is it a failure if you get as close as possible to the center without actually hitting it precisely? I don't think so. Without the goal in the first place you wouldn't even be on the target.

If your goal is to make a million . . . and you only make half a million, don't beat yourself up too much.

– Vince Stanzione

5. Goals must be positive.

A positive goal contains words like "am" or "have" or "own." They are powerful words stating something which you HAVE, not *will have* soon. They are *commands*. Do not confuse this wording with stating the opposite, even though logically the outcome should be the same. Saying, "I am a positive person" is not the same as saying, "I am not a negative person." You don't "give up" smoking. You "live a healthy lifestyle." Speak from abundance, not from scarcity. God said, "Let there be light" not, "Let there be less darkness."

Over many years it has become known that the subconscious mind acts on what you focus on most of the time, irrespective of whether it's what you want. If you're focusing on *how to get out of debt*, you're still focusing on –you've guessed it – debt. If there is something you want or need, then state it positively. If there is something you want to be rid of, then phrase it positively. Leave out negative words like "not," "give up," "never," etc.

I once suffered an allergy that brought me out in spots every spring. It started when I was 17 and continued until I was 35. Doctors put it down to stress (wrong), shellfish (I hated shellfish), and finally eggs (still wrong). Finally I went to a specialist clinic who told me with surprising honesty that they didn't know what it was. It could have been a combination of anything. They gave me some pills to help with the symptoms if not the cure.

I decided that goal-setting was the only solution. I set myself the goal of "I am a very healthy person, full of energy." Each morning and each night I repeated this goal and visualized myself in a state of glowing good health. What I did *not* do was to phrase the goal "I do not suffer from allergies any longer." The phrase "I do not want" is a negative statement and it would have made me focus on the allergy, which is not the correct way.

On the other hand the positive assertion "I AM" is very powerful and the subconscious is commanded to respond, so always remember the difference between a positive statement, or command, and a negative wish or hope.

I put this one goal on the very top of my list. I repeated it faithfully every day, and used the "letting go" technique you will see later every day as well. I was absolutely determined to get rid of it once and for all.

To be honest I don't remember how many weeks it took. I think it was about 15 or 20 at the most, but from that day to this, on my word of honor, I have never had a single reoccurrence of that allergy. I have been free of it now for over 20 years. I have done this trick several times with other chronic health problems and achieved success every time.

6. The goals must be read, preferably rewritten, at least twice a day, every day.

Once you've written down your positive goals, the sheet of paper or card on which they have been written becomes your lifelong friend. Every morning, immediately on rising, find a quiet place and take out your goal sheet. Read out these goals by miming the words with your lips. Better still, read them out loud. The best way is to rewrite them on another piece of paper, but an alternative is to pretend to write it out in thin air, using an invisible pen. Alternatively, write your goals in a computer file. Do the same thing at night before you go to bed.

The object here is repetition. By repeating your goals, you are *driving* these new commands deeply into your subconscious, which will then be re-programmed to achieve those goals. It is very important to take time out, even if it is only a few minutes, and repeat these goals every morning and every night without fail, no matter how tired you may be. The reward will be well worth it. Doing this often enough makes it an experience. The subconscious mind is not able to distinguish between an imaginary experience and a real one. If it's real, then the world, the universe, *must* contain it.

7. After each reading, visualize your life as it would be with that goal achieved. See, in your mind's eye, the new car parked in the drive, smell its interior. Feel excited. Do this for each goal.

Remember to see yourself *as if the goal was already yours*. Feel the excitement. See yourself in the car. See yourself meeting your ideal mate. Yes, that works too. These techniques set up a homing beacon, creating your wants in your life: changing your life. In the case of finding partners it is doubly effective, because that partner is also looking for *you*. Remember, it's not the goal itself that does anything. IT IS THE EMOTION THAT PROVIDES THE POWER TO MAKE GOALS HAPPEN. Don't just read out a goal, feel the same buzz you'd have if it had come true this morning.

Whatever your goal, make certain that you imagine it as being true in your life right now. Get excited. Feel good about it. Don't forget, this is not idle dreaming, you're actually ordering this goal into your life as if from a cosmic catalogue. Have faith in it. Even as I am writing this, remembering the many goals I have achieved, I am amazed and excited at how such a simple idea can bring such magical results.

If you are visualizing a physical goal, then "see" the car, or the house in detail. If it's a holiday on a Pacific island, then see yourself looking at a glorious sunset. "Feel" your feet in the surf.

If you are visualizing a psychological goal – for example, confidence – then "see" yourself in a situation in which you are showing great confidence, such as when giving a speech or talking to the CEO of your corporation. Feel good about it.

8. Don't let the goal own you.

I hope you will understand this section because I suspect you will never have seen it before. Before you finalize your goals I want you to reread this section. These are powerful words of wisdom concerning goal-setting that you must understand before you make a big mistake.

Goal-setting contains two elements that seem to be contradictory, and you must find a balance between them. The object of any goal is simply to make you happier. If *trying to achieve* the goal makes you a stressed-out, anxious person, then rethink the goal.

For each goal you want to achieve, ask yourself this question: "How do I feel about the goal itself?" This means, what feelings come into your mind when you think about this goal? The obvious feelings will be excitement or joy. Think about these feelings and write them down.

Now ask yourself a different question: "How does this goal make me feel *now*?"

Note that the two questions are not the same. The second question refers to your feelings concerning the *attainment* of the goal, the height you have to climb. If your goal was to conquer Mount Everest, then the first question addresses how you think you would feel at the top of the mountain, and the second question addresses how you feel about the whole prospect of organizing the expedition. Think very carefully about this.

So, the first question is "How do I think I will feel *when I have attained* this goal?" and the second question is "How do I feel about this future goal *right now?*"

If today's thoughts concerning your goal make you feel anxious or disturbed or stir hidden doubts *right now*, then think carefully about that goal. What is happening is that deep down a part of you that "knows" is telling you things are not what they seem to be. This goal you have for yourself may be an illusion. You MUST take on board the notion that there is a force outside of yourself that wants the best for you. It wants you to live a life filled to the brim with an unlimited abundance of good things. It will guide you away from bad things, or things you think you want but won't actually make you happy. Be prepared to change your goals away from things you think you want, to things that make you feel good.

Money or financial goals can be a trick. Money isn't a goal; it's a *route* to a goal, and only one route at that. Bypass money and go straight to what you want that money for. That's your real goal. "Financial freedom" is the goal-setting equivalent of "warm and sunny." What do you mean by it? You will have to think of these things.

A great tip is to imagine your ideal life as if it were true today. So if you want to work a few days each week from home and have plenty of free time to walk the beach, then this is a worthy and well thought out goal. If there is a particular car or house you'd like, then describe it in detail, exactly as if you were ordering it. You can't, for example, have a goal of a beach house in Florida if you won't get on the Internet and take a look at some houses in that area.

Think of it this way. Suppose you have just won the lottery. With all that money in the bank you'd go looking for your house, wouldn't you? Of course you would. Well, if you don't start looking at houses after you have made a goal of getting one, what is *that* saying about your commitment, or your belief? You have to *do* something. It kick-starts your ambition and underwrites your intention.

Your subconscious mind is a three-year-old genie. It will create any goal you want, provided it is so clear and unambiguous that any three-year-old could understand it.

But how can you con yourself? It's easy. It starts by basing your goals on the wrong assumptions. The most obvious false assumption is that other people will admire, respect, or love you more because you have this goal. Wrong. Never, ever set yourself a goal that you think will make you feel better or happy *just because you can show off or impress another person.*

Many people who have had the thrill of owning a new car have NOT discovered the unalloyed excitement of being the envy of their friends. Instead, they found that they were embarrassed by it in the company of their friends or worried about it in case it was scratched in the supermarket parking lot.

The fact is that what you *think* will impress another person never will because most people equate "impress" with "envy." *Never let others decide your happiness* because if you do, *they own you.* You will be a willing slave to what you think they want. Be true to yourself.

Let your inner voice tell you what you want. If the thought of trying to achieve any of your goals makes you feel unhappy *now*, then you'll feel exactly the same way in *now + 1 second* and exactly the same in *now + 2 seconds*. Each *now* is the seed of the next *now* and if you are not happy with your goals *now* then you won't be happy *at any time in the future* because each moment you live in is the seed of the next.

Phew . . . that was heavy.

If you think that being a millionaire will make you happy, then study the lives of the many millionaires and celebrities who have committed suicide over the years and ask yourself why. External things, at best, can only make you slightly happier; they cannot make you a truly happy, self-fulfilled person who cares not one jot whether it rains today because you're having a whale of a time, whatever the weather.

Make your goals what *you alone* want them to be. The easy part is achieving the goal. The hard part is deciding which goals are worth the effort, and whether they really are what you need to make you happy.

An obvious financial goal is to earn a certain sum of money. But in today's world we are not paid in cash, and it's very difficult to visualize 100 grand. You can hardly get excited over a bank statement, so if you have difficulty getting excited over an imaginary bank statement, let other goals *allude* to your income goal. To want 100K income but dream of a brand-new VW Beetle doesn't match up unless you are very laid back. The Beetle is telling your subconscious that you don't really believe 100K is attainable. Concentrate on your house and car – the income to achieve those things will often take care of itself.

9. The power of doing nothing

Reading and visualizing your goals twice a day is a practical, active process. However, in mental work we must also remember the sheer power of letting go and letting your mind do its own work. Remember that in *mental* work, the more you strain at the job the less you will get done. Your goal readings are crucial, practical steps, but now we must let the mind continue the good work in its own way. Let the subconscious get on with it. All your conscious mind has to do is make each goal clear, certain, and unambiguous. The subconscious does not require the help of your pathetically weak conscious efforts.

You should "let go" once a day, every day, for about 20 minutes or so. I find the best place is in my parked car, even if I have to drive to some reasonably quiet place to do it. Whenever, and wherever, do this every day.

Close your eyes and spend five minutes relaxing with your eyes closed. Counting slowly backwards from 50 usually achieves the desired result. Once you are in this quiet, totally relaxed state, repeat quietly to yourself your most important goal, and then drift along as you visualize yourself in a situation where this goal is true.

This technique uses the capacity of the mind to inject an idea from the conscious, straight into the subconscious area of the brain, and it is extremely powerful. When you try this technique for the first time you will find it so restful that you may start to fall asleep. Do not worry. You will find that after about 20-40 minutes you will have an almost overwhelming desire to wake up again. Do it. Do not try to doze further, otherwise you will feel dreadful. Just get up and get on with the day.

Another way to understand the power of letting go is to remember the times when you were trying to solve a particular problem, say a math problem. You'd focus on the problem for hours probably, without a result. Finally you would leave it unsolved. The next day the answer came to you unexpectedly, say while walking the dog or washing the car. It came to you after you'd let go. You had spent time focusing on it consciously, and this impressed itself on your subconscious computer. The solution came when your subconscious worked on it but only when it was free to act, i.e., not cluttered up with conscious musings.

All you have to do is to follow the same system and focus on your want, then consciously pass it over to "the powers that be" in the confident expectation that an answer will appear.

It's a no-effort process.

A summary of the best methods to use

1. Write out your goals.
2. Every morning read them out to yourself and visualize them. Feel the buzz. Play some inspiring music on your MP3 player.

3. Take in an encouraging chapter from one of the many self-development books or audio tapes/CDs/DVDs available.
4. At lunchtime, let yourself go in the "power" state of deep subconscious conditioning.
5. Just before retiring, read out your goals and visualize them.

Do not be afraid to change your goals if for any reason the desire for a particular goal seems to wear off. This is because you have an inner power that wants the best for you, and it will suggest new goals, or modify old goals in order to bring you the inner peace that you desire. Go with the flow.

You will also find that new ideas will leap into your head in order to help you achieve those goals. Don't ignore them. Write them down and leave them for a few days so that your thoughts can settle, then look at them again to see if they "feel" right. If they do, then act on them right away. If you get into the habit of ignoring them, they will no longer appear.

Once you get tuned in to this kind of goal-setting you will find the power at work drawing ideas, events, even people towards you. You are moving universes. Use your common sense to identify the best ideas and go with them. That's what your conscious mind is for. If you continuously ignore the workings of your subconscious mind, it will simply become less effective.

Using your goals

You don't have to limit the number of goals you choose, but keep them manageable. Now I'll give you an excellent technique which will help enormously with regard to the very first goals you should choose for yourself. Doing what I am about to say will tell your mind that you mean business in a big way.

1. First of all, write out your goals on a rough sheet of paper until you are happy with the phrasing. Use some of those goals shown later on in this book by all means, but make absolutely certain they are the goals you want, not what you think somebody else would like you to have. Do not try to impress anyone. Don't try to impress yourself. And for heaven's sake have some fun with it; otherwise, what's the point?

2. You should have three psychological goals – personality traits you want to have. These should be for confidence, perseverance and courage. For example:

    "I am a very confident person. Each day my confidence increases."
    "I always finish each task to the very end, without distraction, procrastination or deviation."
    "I am a courageous person. I believe in my capacity to meet all life's challenges head on."

3. Once you have defined three psychological goals, list three simple *physical* goals that you have been putting off for ages. Start with that job in the house or garage you've always wanted to do but never got around to. Have a "fix something" day or talk to your boss about something you've been wanting to for ages. Or take a long weekend break. Treat yourself. Pick anything that *you know is achievable* and create *a firm deadline* for its achievement. You are allowed to have a deadline on a clearly achievable goal because there is no risk of failure. You

are also allowed to have fun. Technically these are not goals, they are management projects, but they will get you into the flow of setting plans and following them through.

These are your *preliminary goals*. As you achieve them one by one, you will be doing two very important things. First, you will be getting into the winning habit. You *will* achieve these goals, and these smaller goals give you the confidence to move on to the big ones. They are not that difficult. They're not supposed to be, but they will give you the experience of creating and achieving a goal. When you achieve any goal you've set yourself, draw a straight line through this goal on your goal-sheet and write the word ACHIEVED after it. Then record it. Your diary will build up into a sizeable success folder, and reading it every now and again will give you renewed confidence.

Second, you are training your mind. You are setting the seal that you mean business. Remember that your mind does not want change. It wants the old status quo because it's safe. It wants you to do more of what you have already done.

If you do more of what you've already done you'll just get more of what you've already got.

– Sign seen at a university campus

By setting goals you are telling your mind that you are not happy with the present situation and you are determined to press the override button.

In the meantime your mind will do everything it can to stop you from achieving these simple goals. Make a note that this will happen.

This is homeostasis. Your mind will set up all kinds of obstacles to hinder your commitment to visualizing them twice a day. Suddenly the bed will be very comfortable to stay in. You'll want to watch that midnight movie and be so tired at the end of it that you just crawl straight into bed. Your work will expand to fill the lunchtime break. Know this, and know this now. *It wants you to fail.* It is setting up some simple diversions to test you. *It is testing your resolve.* If you win, it will get the message and work with you. If you lose . . .

You now have, on rough paper, at least three mental goals and three simple physical goals. After years of working with many people, I can thoroughly recommend to you your first three physical goals AFTER you've achieved the simple preliminary goals mentioned above:

1. Set a goal for a new car.
2. Set a goal for a new house.
3. Set a goal for a certain income.

I know. I've just contradicted myself. Income isn't a goal, and it's very hard to visualize cash. No, I base these goals on exactly what I did when I needed it. Let me explain.

Many years ago, I found myself unemployed. I'd had a falling-out with my business partners. I had no income, little savings, and two small mouths and a big mortgage to feed. Sensibly, what's the first goal you think any reasonable person would have set themselves?

Surely some kind of income goal? Well, I didn't. I decided I'd have a Range Rover. And my lady agreed with me.

The reasons were clear. The car was the upmarket version of the one I'd had in my old business, and the idea of having a nicer car was very exciting because it would have allowed me to give the big finger to my ex-partners should I ever meet them. (*Revenge is a meal best served cold*.) Second, it was something that allowed me to get my confidence back. I had been badly mauled and needed a huge confidence boost. A "successful" car would do just that. It was my version of *Terminator III* – "I'm back!"

The goal was written: "I own a brand-new Range Rover SCE V8i in dark blue with air conditioning, alloy wheels, tow pack, cruise control, ABS brakes, and a five-speed stick shift." This was a serious machine – over $100K, and not a small goal for someone who had just signed a school meals form showing his projected annual income as zero.

So where was the money for all this? It didn't matter. I didn't care what kind of universe was created so long as this car was in it and in my garage (actually it wouldn't fit *in* the garage). This is an important point I will make later: Let the cash take care of itself.

Notice also the phrase: *I own*. This means I owned it. It wasn't rented, borrowed, or a car I had the use of. It was *my* car.

I forget the exact time frame, but within about 18 months *that* car was in my driveway. And I owned it. Universes don't change overnight – but change they do.

Now here's the power of it all and I promise you this is absolutely true. On the day I bought the car, the dealer told me that cruise control was not available with the five-speed manual gearbox, only auto. I don't like autos (control freak). So I said, "*Jeep* do a stick shift with cruise control . . ." One phone call later and the agent located the *only* Range Rover in the country with cruise control and a stick shift. It was a one-off special model built by Land Rover. And guess what color it was? Dead right – dark blue. Over 23 colors to choose from, and the only car in the country with that package was exactly as I visualized it: dark blue.

My house was exactly the same. One week before buying a certain house, the deal fell through. I'd sold my old house, so I had to move quickly. We fell upon a house that had been empty for six months, and it was almost exactly as I had visualized it. Indeed, in every way it's far better. It was waiting for us.

Quantum goal-setting

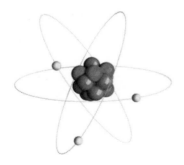
I have a book that was written in 1923. In it there are a couple of paragraphs in which the writer refers to cellular phones and video recorders. Clearly, these must have been added later by well-meaning compilers who simply wanted to clarify the old-fashioned text and make it simpler for modern readers.

In the same way, ancient goal-setting techniques have been changed over the years by well-meaning people who were trying to clarify them for modern audiences. In addition, they assumed that goal-setting was a mainly psychological process, with time management thrown in for good measure. Unfortunately, they threw the baby out with the bath water, so to speak.

Quantum theory and nuclear physics are all about energy. The universe and the big bang theory are all about energy. Matter, what you, I, and everything else is made of, is energy-made-visible. We can't actually see energy, only what it does when it's released or what it looks like when it's converted, temporarily, into matter. In the beginning there was God, and God is energy with personality. The "personality" part is what the great religions of the world are dealing with, and that is outside the scope of this book. We'll get to energy later. Goal-setting is energy conversion.

Goal-setting is easy if you bear two things in mind:

1. The goal must be written out using words that show, conclusively, that this goal has already been achieved. It's a done deal. There is no "I will have"; it is "I have." Period. You are "thinking from the end" as Wayne Dyer puts it. You have a clear vision that this goal is already there.

2. Keep it simple by focusing on things over which you have control. These things are:

   A. Physical things: cars, homes, boats, and money
      – if you realize that money is not a goal in itself.

   B. Do not try to change other people's minds. They have their own goals/dimensions/universes. You cannot make a goal for someone else. You may think you are a singer greater than Johnny Cash, but trying to alter the views and goals of 200 million people who think you're not will be beyond the power of your own belief.

C. The exception is romance. Visualizing someone to love who also loves you requires you to simply combine your goal with someone who has the same goal already. This becomes very powerful as two people are focused on the same goal.

D. Yourself. You have control over your own thoughts and feelings, which is why the three psychological goals are both effective and important. So is health.

Set out on your goal-setting by performing a ceremony that serves to imprint the importance of this in your mind at the very start. All great stages in your life are marked by ceremony, and this is a great stage.

Use the best sheets of writing paper you have, even if you had to buy them specially, and you will write down your first goal, which is:

I have the power to do anything I want to do. I create my own world.

Now return to your goal sheet and write down the psychological goals you have previously set yourself in draft form. Then write down your simple preliminary goals, and finally your main goals. You can have any number, but make sure that they are in harmony with each other and don't conflict.

1. Confidence
2. Determination
3. Courage
4. Fix the fence
5. Fix the car
6. Talk to your father
7. New Porsche
8. New house
9. World cruise

When you have written out your goals on this special piece of paper, copy them out individually onto smaller cards, one goal per card. Then burn the original sheet outside somewhere, while offering this prayer:

As these goals become energy, so my energy becomes reality.

From that great day, and for every day that follows, find time first thing in the morning and last thing at night. Sit somewhere private and quiet and recite each goal; "handwrite" it in the air and finally visualize this goal *as if it had already been achieved*, WITH EMOTION. I think the word *emotionalize* is better than *visualize*. You can always find a photo of the thing you want but seeing it will not work by itself. You have to feel. You need to feel the glow of achievement, even if it's only in your mind. Your mind is where it all starts, and it boils down to feelings.

A GOAL IS NOT A GOAL; IT'S A VOW.

This is a vital point. The success or failure of any goal depends entirely on how much you believe in it. It is driven by the passion behind it. Goals are not to be trifled with. You should regard goals as personal vows.

Sam's will was set; and only death would break it.

– J. R. R. Tolkien, *The Lord of the Rings*

Now *that's* a vow.

With each goal that you achieve, and you WILL achieve them, write ACHIEVED on that card and create a new goal on another card. File the old card in a secret place and refer to your steadily increasing stack of achieved goals whenever you feel the need to do so.

With this system you will be setting very powerful forces in motion on your behalf. Exactly how some of these forces work no one knows or understands. Some are completely outside current scientific explanation. Many come from quantum mechanics, which is a world that is currently completely unknown to anyone except expert scientists or well-informed laymen. Even they don't see the real-life connections – that whatever works in individual cells must also work in the whole body, and what works at atomic levels must also work on a larger scale.

Do not be alarmed or consider these forces as "supernatural." They are very natural. I believe them to be God-given tools necessary for our survival. Like any tool they can, and will be, misused. This does not make the tool evil, just the user.

Goal-setting works by reprogramming and harnessing the subconscious mind power that is currently being used to keep you in your place. How each goal will be achieved varies according to the goal. Psychological goals will be achieved through a process of belief only. With each visualization you are forcing your subconscious to believe that the event you are imagining actually happened. The event then becomes part of you. So by imagining an event in which you showed great courage, and imagining it with passion over a period of time, then you have in effect really lived out that event in real life and therefore believe, absolutely, that you have courage. It's the belief that makes it so.

When you start to believe that you have "the power," then the power within will simply be released to do its healing work. So many people suffer from self-fulfilling failure. They don't believe they have the power within, so that power is never released for positive results.

Physical goals will be different according to the goal. As in the case of the bike or the parking lot experiment, I believe that you have the power to partially influence another person's behavior by thought alone[4]. The parking space often appears because someone is just leaving it. Coincidence? I don't think so. The statistical chances of so many coincidences happening one after the other are against it. Telepathy? Maybe, but not in the usual sense. I believe that all life is interconnected (Dr Lyall Watson's conclusion) in ways that we haven't even dreamed about yet. You can actually draw like-minded people into your life. You can "engineer" coincidences. By making a firm irrevocable decision that something is true, it becomes true in a universe of your making. You will come to believe that there are no such things as coincidences.

---

[4] Generally speaking, quantum goal-setting is brilliant for creating physical things in your life. But it will only affect how *people* respond to you in certain ways. See later.

One of the main ways that goals will be achieved is by "receiving" ideas "out of the blue," ideas that are routes to achieving your goal. I have obtained two cars by using the laws of goal-setting, and in both cases I achieved them simply by changing the way I worked.

My first "ideal" car seemed a pipe dream as I sat underneath the staircase of my first little house banging away in my spare time doing a "teach yourself writing" course. The course didn't make me a penny but shortly afterwards a friend suggested a business idea, then one thing led to another, and car No. 1 was achieved in about 12 months.

The second was much quicker. Initially I couldn't justify the cost of it to the other partners in my business. Eventually, through a strange set of circumstances, the other partners actually suggested it to me.

What happens is that you get ideas for achieving your goal; also, certain helpful events or circumstances or the right people are drawn (or created) into your life. Act on them.

Examples of good, well-worded goals

Only you can decide which goals are meaningful to you, and that's the hardest part. If you really want more money, fine. If you want to be free of money and just beachcombe your life away, fine. Other than telling you that money won't make you happy, just happ*ier*, I'll just offer these examples of well-worded goals which are exactly that: well-worded examples. I give no weight at all to the virtues or vices of any of them. That's your decision. But know that whatever you choose, that's what you will get. Some of these goals are mine.

Others were written by others – and I wish they were mine. They are all good.

Serenity. I am a calm, cheerful person, unflustered by the tides of life.

Self-liking. I love myself. I am a wonderful person and a great and loyal friend.

Speaking. I am an excellent speaker. I speak with authority.

Relaxation. I am always relaxed in all situations.

Courage. I have the courage to face and defeat fear. This courage gives me enormous strength each day.

Perseverance. I always finish each task to the very end, without distraction, persevering always and in all circumstances. In so doing I always obtain results.

Honesty. I am an honest and ethical person.

Success. I am a truly successful person. I am free to create my own world from the wonderful law of abundance shown in nature. I am nature. I am abundance. Success is attracted to me.

Car. I own a brand new, red, Ford Flashbox GLX 2.8i with beige leather upholstery . . . (full details).

Romance #1. I am blessed with my true bride. She is slim, petite, caring, with dark hair and brown eyes that are only for me.

Romance #2. My man is in my life. He is tall, dark, and handsome with blue eyes; he is a faithful partner, a soft, gentle lover, and my best friend.

Money. (Get money in perspective first.) Money comes easily and copiously into my life from many sources in many unexpected ways.

Work. I work three days a week from a small home office, earning all that I need to live my life in any way I choose.

Education. I continue to educate myself on a daily basis, always alert to new ideas.

Health. I abound with good health. I awake with new life energy each day. I see myself as a healthy person.

Attractiveness. I am an attractive, likeable person, always making new friends.

Morning goals: Today is a GREAT day. Today I feel GOOD. This day, wonderful things will happen in my life.

DO NOT TELL ANYONE ABOUT YOUR GOALS, YOUR PLANS, OR ANYTHING TO DO WITH YOUR DREAMS FOR THE FUTURE, not even your nearest and dearest UNLESS they are doing it with you and give you their 100% support. Anyone else will drag you down.

They will ridicule you. They will do it nicely and in "your best interests" because they don't want you to lose any of your hard-earned cash. They will give you 10 reasons why something won't work. If this is the attitude of the people you most closely associate with, then you will effectively be on the receiving end of *their* goals and you will be like them – forever. It's an interesting thought that the biggest critics of self-improvement, those who ridicule it and call it hokum, are almost always not very well paid, and/or not very well liked, and/or not very happy. Avoid them; they want to clip your wings. Do not follow lemmings.

ALWAYS, ALWAYS, ALWAYS inspire yourself daily by reading or listening to some kind of encouraging or motivational CD, DVD or book. Fill your home with such things and refer to them at least once every day.

Do you need money to achieve a goal?

Eight weeks before writing this I saw a TV program in which a man had moved from nothing to a $2 million property in three moves.

At the age of ten his father had driven him down a certain road full of houses normally frequented by minor film stars, pro-footballers, and the like. Serious real estate. At this tender age he decided he would one day buy a house on that same road.

He grew up to be a nightclub manager (not the owner, so his income was average). His first house was very small and he sold it at a profit. He did the same thing with his second house. After two sales he had approximately $100,000 to put down, and it was then he decided to put his youthful plan into action. He immediately contacted several realtors to find out if any houses were available on that exact road, and if so, what the price was. The answer was no, and if there had been, the price would be about $2 million.

He was undaunted. His income was $50,000 and he had $100,000 in cash. So he only needed a mortgage of $1,900,000. (Only!) And that's if a house was for sale, which it wasn't.

A week later he had an idea. Instead of buying a luxury home on that street, perhaps some *land* was for sale. He checked out the prices of building a new house to the same specifications as the others in that road and found he could do it for $400,000 – which was affordable with bank loans.

He checked out the entire road. No land, nothing. But one house had a very large plot, and part of that plot was big enough for a new house and land to go with it. So, our man boldly went where no one had gone before and asked the owner of the house whether he would sell the land. No. Nevertheless, our man asked the same question each month for the next five months, until the owner set up a sign saying: *Not For Sale*.

Finally our man admitted defeat and a few days later he was looking at buying a small house when his cell phone rang. Due to a change of circumstance the owner of the large plot was suddenly interested in an offer.

To cut a long story short, our man bought the plot and built the house, all for less than $500,000 based on bank loans. On the day the house was finished he was offered $1,500,000 for it in cash. He refused and for all I know he lives in his $2 million mansion to this day – *and he still earns $50,000 a year as a nightclub manager.* And *that* is the point of this story. Anybody else would have tried to up their income in some way, in order to afford their dream home. He didn't. Today *he* has the home that a thousand others like him could never have afforded.

You don't always need money, so let money take its rightful place in your life – it is not a goal, and sometimes it's not even needed.

A lack of constructive and persistent goal-setting is a goal in itself. It says you will fail.

– James Edwin

Chapter Seven

*I Don't See Millionaires
Making Goal Lists*

WHEN YOU'RE ONE, you may not have to. This book is dedicated to those many people who have unfulfilled wants and desires that seem to elude them, no matter how hard they try. The fact is that successful people don't do the details of what I have written down but they do the *principles* so well, they don't have to. To a successful person, being successful is second nature, part of their psyche, their expectations. To them, the next success is as obvious as selecting Brand X toothpaste and putting it in the cart.

As far as I know, the guy with the $2 million mansion did not write out the goal but he certainly visualized it. He'd visualized it, with passion and belief, since he was 10. It became true, albeit in stages, the moment he *acted*, because in acting he made the *decision*, the absolute commitment necessary to change his universe into a new one. You have to act as well as think.

Successful people have the knack of doing the right thing. They instinctively:

- Have an absolutely clear vision of what it is they want.
- Have an absolute belief they will achieve it.
- Have the courage and determination to just do it.

By contrast, unsuccessful people:

- Don't know what they want. This is quickly proven when I ask them what their number one goal is. They don't know. Also, they don't have any details. It's all about "warm and sunny." (By contrast I have yet to meet a successful person who couldn't tell me, in mind-numbing detail, what their next project – or goal, same thing – is about.)

- Don't really believe they can do it. They *say* they do but *believe* they can't – and therefore they can't.

- Lack determination. As a result, they only give anything a halfhearted stab and run for cover at the first sign of a problem. This is not their fault. Much of this is the result of a less-than-perfect educational system and less-than-perfect role models at home.

Imagine successful people to be car drivers and unsuccessful people to be walkers. Once walkers have taken the driving lessons, with each mile they drive they become more confident. Most drivers do not need to go through the basics every time they get in the car. They just drive. Learners have to learn. Once you have achieved a certain level of personal success (and it's only you who defines what level that is) then much of what you do after that is on autopilot.

What if I want one thing, but my wife/spouse/life-partner wants something else?

This is difficult. You cannot make goals for others. Even if you compromise, this watered-down goal may not give you the same passion you would have for your own goal. You can't fool yourself, not deep down.

If you want a two-seater Italian sports car but you have four kids, then I'd suggest a goal of two cars. But if I wanted a house in town, and my wife wanted a house in the middle of nowhere, then I'd sit down and have a looooong talk about it. You can't have everything if you have others to consider.

What if she makes a firm goal for house A and you make a firm goal for house B? Then you may well end up in different houses, if you know what I mean. However, you could make a goal of having two houses, and spend time in each.

When does true belief in yourself drift into delusion?

Most of us have seen TV shows where hopefuls audition to be the next pop star. Some of these hopefuls go from audition to audition, full of belief that they are great singers just waiting for the right break to come along. The reality is that they are unutterably dreadful singers who have deluded themselves into star status. But if they believe it, in a quantum world, why aren't they stars?

I could answer that in *their* (small) world, they *are* stars. The problem is that no one else outside their world sees it. All the goal-setting I have demonstrated above involves either changing yourself (psychological goals) or attracting/creating physical things like houses and cars, which by themselves have no desire to change. (A car is a car.)

When it comes to influencing others, I believe it becomes more complex because other people unwittingly have their own universes filled with preconceived ideas of what is good or bad: the human core program. This goal-setting system works brilliantly in attracting, say, a new friend or lover and this is arguably because they are also looking for you, so your goals match. In the case of car parking, I think my desire to have a parking space appear on a certain street and time must match, or influence, someone else's decision to leave that spot. On the other hand, it may not. See Appendix C.

I think the boundary of most people's influence encompasses physical objects, similar-minded people, or neutral-minded people. Indeed, except where other people are in tune with our wants and desires, we have little control outside of "our own little world." You could envisage this with the core program analogy I made at the beginning. You can't change the world, only your part in it.

But what you can do, most certainly, is to take control of those things that matter to you.

The object of success engineering is to set out, on paper, a blueprint of those things you want. Most often this narrows down to:

- physical things
- type of work
- love and relationships
- health

For the vast majority of people, to have a nice car, nice house, plenty of free time, productive enjoyable employment, romance, and financial freedom is all we want. It's not a lot to ask, not really. So why not just engineer these things?

* * *

We all have two choices: to make a living, or design a life.

Chapter Eight
Advanced Weird Stuff

Why all this is being taken very seriously

I KNOW ALL this quantum stuff sounds strange, but a great deal of money is going into this. Why? And if it's all theory and nonsense, why should you or anyone else believe a word of it?

Well, one day a group of scientists went up to the Pentagon asking for research money. They said, "Gentlemen, we have a situation where qubits, being quaternary in nature, differ from the laws of classical physics in that they exist in a superposition of classical states representing the probability of each state. We now envisage being able to execute a 'Controlled-NOT' operation simultaneously on 2^{500} states derived from massive parallelism and achieve the equivalent of the same operation as a classical computer on 10^{150} separate processors, which, of course, is impossible in a classical framework but . . ."

At which point the military gentlemen interrupted, and after formulating a fulsome and erudite response said, "Huh?"

The scientists went into a huddle and finally rephrased the situation in terms a chimp could understand. "There is a new technology that will render every computer, every security code, every security system in the United States obsolete overnight. The first country or organization, friendly or otherwise, perfecting this will have the entire United States military, government, and banking system entirely at their mercy."

To which the military explored the outer limits of their of their linguistic ability and said, "Oh, ****!"

"Unless," continued the brains, "we come up with it first. Then every *other* computer, every *other* security code, every *other* security system in the world will be at our mercy."

"How much do you want?" said the military.

So you see, some very big people are taking all this weird stuff very seriously. But what's the big hoo-ha?

The secret, your Majesty, is for the enemy to only discover those secrets we mean him to discover.

– Benjamin Disraeli

Secrets we mean him to discover . . .

Deciding how much freedom you want to keep for yourself and how much freedom you are prepared to relinquish for the common good is becoming more and more difficult. This is because any method you choose to make yourself invisible to others can also be used by some very serious and scary bad guys, people who would not hesitate for one instant to wipe you and me off the face of the earth for no reason whatsoever, as we know only too well. And some of those aren't even governments. You have to be very careful with your selection of freedoms. Fortunately you can now choose to take quite a lot of freedom as your right, due to two things: the new dependence on computers (both as a storage and communication medium) and Mr. Philip Zimmermann.

There is no better example of someone who is both saint and sinner than Philip Zimmermann. The United States authorities, it would be safe to say, would like to lock him up and throw away the key. People who value their freedom, on the other hand, think he's a saint. In reality he's a guy who had to make a hard decision, and whether his solution was good or bad, I'll let you decide for yourself. It's a fascinating story.

Blinding Big Brother

In 1991 Philip R. Zimmermann launched the most important, and disputed, development in software. He distributed it as shareware – free software – for anyone who wanted it. It was called PGP, which stands for Pretty Good Privacy. PGP was the first commercial use of an idea called Public Key Encryption – basically a new kind of unbreakable code.

The original discovery of Public Key Encryption is now correctly attributed to James Ellis, an eccentric and brilliant physicist, together with mathematician Clifford Cocks, both working for GCHQ (Government Communications Headquarters) in the United Kingdom. This information was never released because the research fell under the U.K. Official Secrets Act. Four years later in the United States, Public Key Encryption was rediscovered completely independently and equally brilliantly by Martin Hellman, Ralph Merkle, and the delightfully named Whitfield Diffie.

Their project was to create an unbreakable computer code. Phil Zimmermann didn't invent this code-creating technology; what he did was to create a practical version of it that anyone could use. This he called PGP – a software program that encrypts (codes) a computer file in such a way that it is almost impossible to crack the code except by using very powerful computers, for a very long time. The effect that PGP had on "locking" computer files beyond the reach of others is best described by Bruce Schneier, in his book Applied Cryptography:

There are two kinds of cryptography in this world: cryptography that will stop your kid sister from reading your files, and cryptography that will stop major governments from reading your files. This book is about the latter.

PGP was a practical application of this new coding or encryption technology. It brought theory and higher mathematics together in a simple software package that did all the encryption automatically within seconds, allowing anyone who used it complete computer and email privacy. Phil Zimmermann had to decide whether to give this software to the FBI or sell it (in which case the FBI would probably have impounded it) or simply give copies away for free, in which case once even one copy was free on the Internet, it was impossible to stop. He chose the latter – and when the U.S. authorities found out about it they caused him several years of grief, trying to imprison him for all kinds of spurious reasons. But that's another story.

In one simple action Zimmermann not only allowed everyone on the planet to lock their computer files and email messages beyond all snoopers (a good thing) but, of course, he also allowed the bad guys to do exactly the same (a bad thing). Whether this was the right decision or not only history will judge.

The combination of Messrs. Hellman, Merkle, Diffie, and Zimmermann allowed information kept on computers to be secure, not only on their own, but secure when unleashed on the Internet. Indeed any credit card transaction enacted over the Internet would be impossible were it not for these pioneers. They created eCommerce. They also created every computer security system on the planet.

Breaking the code

$$\int_a^b f(x)\,dx = F(b) - F(a)$$

It is, in fact, remarkably easy to break this computer code. It works on the basis of a simple formula: $p \times q = N$ where N is a very large number and p and q are two prime numbers. This is high school stuff.

Well, no, actually. It's high school stuff provided N is a small number, much like the example I gave you earlier about how a computer works out the square root of nine. But if N gets very large, say in the region of 10^{130}, then we have a problem because it would take forever to work it out.

Of course, if you had 10^{130} computers available with nothing better to do, then all of them working on just a piece of the process would fling out the answer immediately.

You're ahead of me, aren't you? If there's only 10^{89} atoms in the universe you cannot get the number of classical computers necessary to do the calculation. BUT a quantum computer could set up 10^{130} quantum computers, each in its own universe, and do all the math in a split second.

So now you see why all this quantum stuff is very important – and that's why some very intelligent people are working on a solution to getting a quantum computer up and running. Check out "quantum computer" on any search engine to see how much effort is going into this. Why? Because it's going to change your life, whether you like it or not.

No one gets to vote on whether technology will change their lives.

– Bill Gates

I simply mention this as evidence. All this business of multiple universes may seem like the fantastic delusion of a strange man who writes books. But facts speak for themselves. Go find a parking space.

Chapter Nine

Me! $= mc^2$

IF YOU WANT some encouragement in your life, read the early history of Albert Einstein. Google it.[5] It is a complete mystery how a low-level, grade three clerk with a history of failed exams and no university degree became the most famous and best-known scientist in history, so there's hope for everyone.

One of his most famous and simplest equations was $E = mc^2$. Millions know of it but have never really worked it out. Let me help you.

It's the formula for working out how much energy you are made of. If you weigh 80 kg (about 176 lbs.) then if we decided to use you for fuel in a nuclear reactor, you would produce, wait for it . . .

240,000 million, million kilowatt-hours of power, which is enough power to run a 3 kW electric fan heater for about 9 million, million years, or longer than the universe has been in existence.

---

[5] Allegedly Google's founder, Larry Page, named the site after the Googol number but got the spelling wrong. It was too late to change it. At the time of writing, Google is arguably the most common spelling error in the English language. Ironically, Google's own spelling checker does not currently correct itself.

Now let's think of this another way. This is the amount of energy that "condensed" into physical form to make YOU. Now that's a whole hunk of energy. So where did it come from?

If you got into your car and drove for 15 miles you'd be in outer space. Of course this requires you to drive vertically upwards, which is a neat trick if you can get away with it without dying. What you'd die of, exactly, depends entirely on your speed.

 If you held your breath for 62 miles you'd freeze to death with alarming speed. The average temperature of deep space is minus 270.3 degrees Celsius. In comparison, liquid nitrogen is a relatively tropical minus 195.8 degrees, and that's enough to turn a rose into something looking like glass, which you can smash with a hammer into a thousand pieces. So after a short vertical drive you would soon take on a glassy-eyed expression in more ways than one, and your frozen grin would drift off into eternity, without touching anything or even knowing of a black hole because there's nothing out there. Nothing at all.

There's nothing out there because the average density of the universe as a whole is one atom per cubic centimeter. Yes, we know of places where it's more dense than that, like the chair you're sitting on, but there's a whole lot more places where there's nothing at all, hence an average of one atom, just one, in a volume the size of a sugar cube.

That's why breathing up there might be a tad tricky, particularly as most of those atoms are hydrogen and you'd have to go a long, long way to get even a glimpse of a distant cousin who knew a friend who owned a hat possibly once belonging to an oxygen atom.

There's nothing out there, guys. Even the stars you see aren't there. That's where they were millennia ago. Today they might not even be in existence. The next time you see the sun just peeking over the horizon, consider that the real sun is about 9.5 minutes higher in the sky than it looks. It takes that long for the sun's light to get here. You've never seen the real sun; you see the one that's 9.5 minutes old.

This atomic density means that the amount of energy out there is also rather low. Indeed it's a hotly debated subject, because the math shows that there's no energy at all. I quote astrophysicist Lawrence Krauss: "There appears to be this energy of empty space that isn't zero!" – meaning that the math shows space to be devoid of all energy, so where is the heat in a heated debate coming from? And, indeed, where did the 240,000 million, million kilowatt-hours of energy needed to make *him* come from, too?

If this energy (which is the only thing that existed before the big bang or anything else) was suddenly changed into matter (and a highly organized and complex arrangement at that) then what caused this energy to suddenly change state? How about – a thought? Usually, nothing happens until someone thinks about what it is that is supposed to happen.

Everything created by humans, from the Empire State Building to cars, to this book, started out as a thought in someone's mind; and without that initial spark of reflection, nothing would have happened. We accept this on a human level without question, but for some reason we cannot accept it on a cosmic level. The simple physical reality of the universe is that everything created is created by the thought of that change. But thinking requires a thinker who thought the thought, and science gets all hung up about that because it's outside their box. Yet thought still precedes action, which precedes change, so possibly on a cosmic level when the thought is sufficiently powerful, energy changes into matter. It's that simple. Ridiculous, but simple.

I find it very interesting that some nuclear physicists, who are perfectly ready to accept 16 new dimensions, can't see what's going on when they dig deeper into the quantum field. The deeper they go, the more complications they need to find answers for, and the desire to "discover" some new particle, a pi-meson, an anti-neutrino, a contra-rotating quark, or a wok-fried eggplant, some*thing*, any*thing* that explains what's going on becomes their predominant thought. They look for new things, not realizing that their very belief that this thing must exist perhaps causes that thing to be created.

They are creating their own nuclear world. They can continue the hunt for a completely Unified String Theory, but will they find it if they have already gone beyond the point where they can find a physical or mathematical solution to a spiritual problem? Like the frog who only ever jumps halfway across the road and therefore gets ever closer to, but never ever reaches, the far side, the solution may always be that one small step away. In an ironic twist, science (in particular nuclear science), which was invented to replace philosophy, has now become more like philosophy than science. The future lies with those physicists like Dr Fred Alan Wolf, Dr John Hagelin, and others who can see the power of mind within creation itself.

"Creating" things that didn't exist before we thought they existed may not just belong to the realm of small things. I am trying to find the exact reference to this, but in the sequel to this book I will try to add flesh to the story of the discovery of the planet Pluto. Dr Percival Lowell was a hugely influential astronomer who in the early 1900s became obsessed with the idea that a ninth planet existed. To cut a long story short, when enough people believed this planet existed, it was discovered on February 25, 1930, by Clyde Tombaugh, who worked at Lowell's observatory. There is nothing in this story to add credence to the idea that Pluto was "created" when enough people thought it existed, but read on.

Apparently, having discovered where Pluto was in space, astronomers at the time calculated where Pluto should have been in the years before it was found and examined the photographic plates of where Pluto should have been then. They couldn't find it. Plates taken of that part of the sky that should have showed Pluto before it was officially discovered didn't show it. Of course, photographic plates in those days did not have the resolution of modern plates so this "obvious nonsense" was put down to irregularities in the plates. Pluto is, after all, very small. Nevertheless, it wasn't on the plates.

Then again, Dr Lowell was convinced (a mental goal) that this planet truly existed and was only waiting to be discovered. His power and influence affected others until finally, it appeared. When it comes to planets, it seems a group of people need to believe something before sufficient belief becomes available to convert energy into matter or change dimensions. It should be added that today, evidence of the existence of Pluto on old photographic plates taken before 1930 does exist, which begs the question of whether those specks were there all along, or appeared when sufficient people expected them to be there? Powerful stuff, this energy thing.

Getting the buzz

Look at your hand. Poke it with the other hand. Looks solid, doesn't it? You wish!

If you got an amazingly efficient microscope to take a picture of your hand you would see the skin start like a mountain range, followed eventually by the skin cells. As your magnification increases the cells would reveal their innards – genes, followed by the very DNA of their construction. Keep going and you'd see large clusters of molecules that make up the DNA. Molecules would eventually give way to individual atoms, which, if you could see them, would appear as fuzzy balls.

They're fuzzy because they aren't balls. They look like our solar system. Uncannily so, in fact. Where we have the Sun, they have a nucleus consisting of at least one particle, called a proton. In orbit around the nucleus, like a planet going around the Sun, we have electrons, roughly one per proton, and each one weighing nearly 1,860 times less and all whizzing around their orbits so fast that they are just a notional blur. And they're not going around in one plane like Saturn's rings; their orbits are spherical, like a high-speed motorcycle stunt team zooming around the inside of a giant sphere. If you want to be really confused, they aren't anywhere at all and, at the same time, everywhere there is.

In the same way that the planet Mercury has a smaller orbit than that of Mars, electrons move in different but preprogrammed distances from the nucleus forming layers of spheres, or shells, like you see when peeling an onion.

Stay with me now, so far this is the easy bit.

Pluto is no longer a planet, having been demoted to a "dwarf planet," a polite way of saying it's little more than a big asteroid. Irrespective of its new designation, it still whizzes around the Sun every 250 years, but it's so far away from the Sun that if you sat on Pluto with a very large telescope looking for it, all you'd get is a view of a slightly brighter dot than most of the others and a stiff neck.

It's the same with electrons. An atom is mostly empty space. Imagine a very big beach ball. The nucleus would be less than the size of a pinhead and the electron would be too small to see whizzing around the surface of the ball. And the skin of the ball is only the first "electron shell." The next onion layer would be about the size of a large tractor tire, and so it goes on.

Let's keep boldly magnifying where no one has magnified before.

Keep going in there and protons, together with their same-sized sister particles, neutrons, start to look big. Then we see the "cells" of the protons, weird things called subatomic particles.

We see quarks of all kinds: up quarks, down quarks, strange quarks, and charm quarks; leptons and fermions with half-integer spins. Muons and positrons, leptons and bosons, gluons and gravitons, and majorons with seesaw mechanisms.

I kid you not. These are real and I haven't even gone down the autobahn of antiparticles yet. But start to dig deeper and we hit another problem. A photon is a particle, and also not a particle because it's a wave . . . sort of. A tachyon both does and does not exist at the same time. It also goes faster than the speed of light, which can't happen (there is no Warp 2 outside of Star Trek but no one's told the Tachyons, it seems). And this is where it gets so weird that it's not beyond the bounds of reason to suspect that somewhere in this subatomic freak show is a wok-fried eggplant-ion just waiting to be discovered.

We've reached the end of matter, the solid stuff. There was no boundary like the medieval edge of the earth, no place where matter ended and weird theories began. Somewhere between a charming quark and Mr. Rush the Tachyon, real things became unreal, things we could see became unseen, and solid stuff became – energy.

Energy has many different forms – different ways in which it can be identified and examined. There's kinetic energy – speed. There's potential energy – speed before it happens. There's gravitational energy, electromagnetic energy, mechanical energy, electrical energy, the "weak" force, the "strong" force, and heat. Light is energy.

If we want to delve deeper into our makeup, we have to leave "stuff" behind and think about energy. And to make a very long story short, we end up (currently) in a place called String Theory, in which everything is made up of energy in the form of vibration. Imagine a circle of string, floating in nothing, and this circle of string has a vibration moving along it, like a jump rope tied in a circle, or a circular violin string.

That's what you are. You're a piece of string tied in a circle vibrating so fast that you'd need to slow it down 2.4×10^{17} times before you could even hear it humming. Everything you see and can't see, every molecule of air you've ever inhaled and exhaled, every star, fingernail, person, pet, mountain, or the hand you're still poking is made up of countless numbers of theoretical hummingbirds fluttering in sea of nothing. You're a vibration. You buzz. Dogs know it. We don't.

Dog training for beginners

If you decided to continue to buzz along a certain street in the warehouse district of downtown Los Angeles at around six in the morning, you might see a diminutive Mexican gentleman going for a walk. He's hard to miss because two of his most distinguishing features are a huge smile and the pack of 20 dogs he has with him. Quite often he's rollerblading, with several of his pack dogs pulling him along like a chariot racer in *Ben Hur*.

His name is Cesar Millan, and if you take a closer look at some of his dogs, you'll notice that they have the look of the prizefighter about them, as if he's taking the doggy mafia out to play. You'll see shredded ears, missing eyes, and unnaturally shortened tails belonging mainly to dogs most people are afraid of – pit bulls, Rottweilers, and German shepherds, to name but a few. Most of these dogs are in rehab. They have either suffered intolerable cruelty from the species that invented the word *civilized*, or were otherwise saved from certain execution by owners who thought they were uncontrollable.

Cesar Millan can walk into a room in which a German shepherd the size of a timber wolf, or a pit bull whose jaw muscles are strong enough to break his own teeth, is terrorizing its owner to the point that they dare not allow strangers into the house. Within seconds this dog will be entirely submissive and quiet, allowing Cesar "control" of the whole room. He will achieve this without saying a word. He very rarely uses the commands "sit" or "down." In the main he makes a noise —"Shusss," or similar — and a dog that's had its own way sometimes for eight or more years becomes obedient and entirely submissive. If you've not seen this before it is very, very impressive, which is why the idiotic celebrity owners of Hollywood's pampered pets constantly hire him to sort out their entirely self-generated problems.

The reason Cesar can regain control of a seemingly insane lupine monster within minutes lies in his ability, like Dr Doolittle's, to speak the universal language of all dogs, if not all animals. That language is, surprisingly, not English (so telling a dog he's a very, very naughty boy makes about as much sense as my writing this in fluent Klingon).

In Cesar's own words, the universal language of all dogs is energy. Every dog has a natural antenna we humans have civilized out of ourselves. And this antenna picks up the energy transmitted by other creatures and allows the dog to read humans like an open book. If the owner is excited, the dog is excited. If the owner is calm, the dog becomes calm. It matters not one jot what the owner says, or even how he or she says it. It's what the owner *thinks* and *feels* that tells the dog instantly how to react. A freaky dog, with very few exceptions, has a freaky human near it who thinks the problem is the dog.

Because I've seen and read about Cesar's work, and because I train dogs myself, I see examples of this all the time. Of particular interest is the true situation concerning the so-called aggressive dog.

Some weeks ago my wife was walking Dexter, our German shepherd, off-lead. In the distance a man approached and about 30 yards away he stopped and called for her to put the dog on a lead. This was because he'd already been attacked by two dogs that morning and quite understandably wanted to keep what was left of his trousers intact. Denise complied and also made Dex lie down, which is a very submissive position for a dog.

As the man walked past he glared at the dog, and it was obvious he was scared stiff. Dexter didn't move because Denise was overriding all this fear-energy with calm, assertive energy. But that's not what usually happens, and this might be of interest to those who are wary of dogs, and it's all to do with energy.

The man was making two classic mistakes. First, his fear was palpable. The dog, indeed Denise, could pick up the signals easily. In the dog world, fear is a prelude to attack. A fearful dog is preprogrammed to attack as a form of defense – a preemptive strike. So Dexter could instantly feel the man was afraid, and because of this fear, Dex's doggie brain decided the man was likely to attack him. To make matters worse, the man was staring at Dexter. This is like a man staring at another man in a bar. It's an aggressive act. So the signals Dexter picked up were, *this man is fearful, therefore likely to attack me, and this man is staring at me, therefore will attack any second.*

You can see now why this man was attacked twice before and will be in the future. He was giving off fear-energy and compounding it by adding an aggressive stare. Other dogs weren't attacking him, they were defending themselves against an imaginary attack to be launched *by him*. The correct way to approach a strange dog is to completely ignore its existence. Do not make eye contact. Turn your back if necessary, and always exude calm, assertive confidence.

What I've done here is what I promised at the beginning of the book – namely, to get away from a subject to see if a different angle can make the view clearer, like looking for a blue object on a blue carpet.

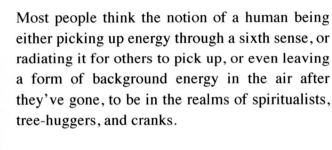

Most people think the notion of a human being either picking up energy through a sixth sense, or radiating it for others to pick up, or even leaving a form of background energy in the air after they've gone, to be in the realms of spiritualists, tree-huggers, and cranks.

And yet the fact that dogs pick up energy signals, and other animals do the same, is well documented. Gazelles and lions often drink at the same time at the same waterhole. The gazelles "know" if the lion is aggressive. They might not know he's just eaten and therefore does not require hors d'oeuvres, but they do pick up the "I'm not interested" energy. Mind you, they still watch him.

And it's not just subliminal signals like stance, smell, or body language that masquerade as energy. There is something else that science cannot define. In his book, *The Dog's Mind*, expert veterinarian Bruce Fogle, D.V.M., M.R.C.V.S., writes of dogs' ability to see and predict events:

The answer . . . lies in the superlative use of the existing senses in conjunction with sensory capacities that we do not as yet fully understand.

So we'll define it. It's energy. But energy is vibration, humming strings, so rather than talking of energy any more, why don't we look at the world through different eyes?

Good vibrations

Instead of seeing ourselves as a physical body, we could equally well see ourselves as a whole heap of kilowatt-hours condensed into one space. Alternatively, we can see ourselves as a zillion googols of superstrings all vibrating in some sort of harmony.

When you hear a symphony orchestra, you tend not to hear the sound of individual instruments but the sound as a whole – a harmony. All the notes made by individual instruments blend to form such a harmony. The vibrations combine to form a new master vibration – a complex waveform – that is the vibration of the orchestra at that moment.

This vibration affects you in more ways than one. The most obvious effect is for you to feel the sound physically, but it also affects you emotionally. Music has the unique power to create mood and feeling. It can make you sad, proud, brave, melancholy, or joyful. It can lift your spirits and make you feel like a different person. One of the best pieces of advice I can give you is to use music to change your mood. By reciting/visualizing your goals and at the same time associating that vision with some stirring music, you can turbocharge your goal creation.

In the same way that a theme from a film stirs me, but may leave you unmoved or even bored, we all not only respond to different "vibrational inputs" but can be said to exist at different vibrational levels, or levels of vibration.

We are each an orchestra playing our own symphony, but some people's idea of a symphony can be very dark indeed, whereas others' is lighter and higher.

Energy, like water, flows from higher levels to lower, from high pressure to low pressure. High pressure air hoses do not suck in air from the surroundings. Water always flows downhill. It's natural law, and because our vibrational level is energy, it must do the same.

There are people you know, perhaps colleagues at work, or friends, or the spouses of friends, whom you try to avoid for reasons you can't quite figure. These people are often friendly and helpful, possibly with hearts of 24-carat gold; they'll do anything for you, and yet you try to avoid them because for some reason you can't quite put your finger on, you leave an encounter with them feeling drained, as if they sucked the energy out of you.

That's exactly what they did. They sucked energy out of you. When someone of high energy – a higher level of vibration – meets someone at a lower energy level, or lower vibration, then energy transference takes place by natural law. The opposite is also true. You can be in a room full of strangers and be drawn to one person whom you have never met or seen before, simply because you feel this urge to either know the person better or just be in his or her presence – to bask in their glow, so to speak. You are quite literally doing so. Certain spiritual, or high energy, or very aware individuals draw like-minded people towards them. By high energy I don't mean some manic arm waver at a rah-rah convention; I mean those souls who genuinely vibrate at a higher level, often doing nothing physical at all. They just are what they are, oases of light in a desert of darkness.

We say we resonate with such people and indeed, we do. You are not a frequency; you are a multitude of frequencies, and to a greater or lesser extent, when you interact with another person, those frequencies interact. When favorable, we resonate with another person; when unfavorable, we don't. Resonance is a powerful creative force in its own right; strike a tuning fork, and as it vibrates, it will cause any nearby fork tuned to the same frequency to vibrate in harmony.

The frequency of love

Denise likes to play cards. I can't stand cards. She likes sailing; I go motor racing. She wants to live in the country; I'm less inclined. She swims like a fish; I sink like a stone. Heights make her feel ill; I can abseil (rappel) off a skyscraper. Judge us as a *future* couple by the degree of things we have in common and you'll probably give the marriage a few years before it fizzles out. And yet we've been together for nearly 30 happy years.

We resonate. When her energy highs match my energy lows, she fills me with power. When she's low-energy, I'm high-energy and I lift her.

We were drawn towards each other years ago because I engineered it. The power of success engineering to draw you to your true love is multiplied thousands of times simply because the person you seek is also seeking you. In a universe full of little else other than vibrations and energy, space and distance is no barrier. In a multi-universe of probability in which a different, personalized version of reality is created the moment a decision is made, the fact that two people are looking for the same version with great passion and intensity is enough to draw them together with scientific certainty. Or create them out of thin air. Or have their universes merge. If you're lonely, just try success engineering on your future soul mate – and be amazed.

The chicken or the egg?

If all this is true (that mind is energy and energy is mind and therefore the mind controls all), then any competent neuroscientist would see a serious fly in this metaphysical ointment. Which came first, the brain or the mind within it?

It's perfectly clear that without a brain (or a dead one) any notion of mind ceases to exist. Furthermore, brain damage produces serious mind damage. The brain is clearly the wiring of the mind in much the same way as a software program runs through the circuitry of a computer chip. Alter or damage the chip, and the program will run improperly if at all. More importantly, the software cannot, by itself, alter the physical circuitry of the chip, which makes it clear that the chip is everything and the software a mere ancillary. But if the software, acting alone, could alter the physical wiring of the chip, then that puts the software in a whole new league altogether.

If the brain is prewired and unalterable, then the mind takes a secondary role. A baked cherry cake stoically remains a cherry cake. It cannot turn itself into a pot of petunias and a bewildered sperm whale by an act of will. If the mind takes such a subservient and secondary role to its own storage area, how can the mind be a thing of its own?

Accepted scientific wisdom – dogma – is very difficult to alter and quite rightly so, for if every small deviation from a scientific truth immediately changed that truth, then there would be no science, only chaos. It's an acceptable irony that science must by its very definition allow freedom of thought and experimentation, whilst at the same time ruthlessly stamp on any new idea until it can not only be proven, but *accepted as proven* in the minds of a majority of the scientific community.

In 1913, the Nobel Prize-winning neuroanatomist Santiago Ramón y Cajal wrote a treatise on the nervous system in which he stated and proved that the nerve paths in the living brain, once "set" by age, are "fixed, ended and immutable." As recently as 1999, neurologists wrote in the journal *Science* that "the fully mature brain lacks the intrinsic mechanisms needed to replenish neurons and reestablish neuronal networks."

What they were getting at is two things. First, brain cells – neurons – are unlike other body cells because they cannot reproduce. If it's broke, it stays broke. You cannot grow or create new brain cells. Second, once the brain networks mature, that wiring stays mostly the same in adult life. Yes, changes can take place, but only at a low level. New "existing" pathways can modify themselves slightly. We can strengthen the odd synapse and caress a dendrite or two in order to allow existing neurons to talk to each other in a new way, much like adding a new phone line. But essentially the brain is fixed like our computer chip and therefore the notion of anything changing it, especially the mind, is nonsense. This, of course, relegates the previous pages of this tome to the realms of fantasy. How can you change a whole universe but not alter that mushy stuff inside your head? That's it, end of story, thanks for buying the book. Goodbye, and thanks for all the fish.

Fortunately for the trees sacrificed in the production of this work, all does not end here. By the middle of the 20th century, the idea of neuroplasticity – a brain that changes – was catching on through experiments by people like the psychologist Donald Hebb, who was promptly ignored by the neuroscientific community simply because he was a psychologist. It shows how brilliant Einstein was. It is not enough to publish a breakthrough; you must have the credentials, the authority, to publish. This of course is pure elitism and completely unscientific, but wherever humans gather, human nature will rule.

Truth and time will conquer. Enter stage left – stem cells, those plucky little subcutaneous Lego bricks that can morph into all sorts of different cells, including neurons. There are powerful ideas developing in this field that throw a serious spanner into the dogma machine. You still cannot replicate neurons, but you can certainly create new ones.

Enter stage right – the Dalai Lama.

Tensin Gyatso is the 14th Dalai Lama and arguably the most influential reformer of Buddhism ever. A basic tenet of Buddhism is the pursuit of truth, and this Dalai Lama has embraced Western scientific discoveries as part of that truth to the extent where, if modern science disproves an idea previously held for thousands of years, then truth is truth and must be embraced.

In 2004 the Dalai Lama hosted a meeting between a group of elite Buddhists – arguably the world's greatest examples of disciplined mental activity – and some of the world's leading neuroscientists in an attempt to combine their knowledge of mind and brain. The outcome, as revealed in Sharon Begley's book *Train Your Mind, Change Your Brain*, is clear from the title.

The old dogma is not just cracking but is being systematically destroyed by new insights and research showing that a disciplined mind clearly can alter the physical conditioning of the very brain that gave birth to it. The program is greater than the chip. The mind is everything.

Scientists free from the bondage of dogma, and journalists like me who try to shake and rattle the piggy bank of science to see if new ideas can be coaxed out of it, are noticing that Buddhism has little to worry about. Without question, some new scientific truths are replacing ancient doctrines, but only Western arrogance would assume that this is one-way traffic. The reality is that a surprising reversal is taking place where ideas, philosophies, and ancient wisdoms are not being erased by science but confirmed. Instead of disproving the mystical, the road of discovery runs parallel with it.

The only things we ever are, have been, or will be, are manifestations of energy, one energy which binds all universes, all decisions, all thoughts together into a whole that is so great, only God or the god-like could ever see it. And yet it seems the humblest mortal has been given the power to use it.

Chapter Ten

Success Engineering

Bud-doiing!

YOU HAVE SEEN it many times. The fly is trapped in the room. It sees the outside, flies towards it, and bud-doiing, head-butts the window. Then, it sees the outside, flies towards it again and bud-doiing, head-butts the same window. It does this hundreds of times with little reward other than a major headache. Of course, the next windowpane along is open, but the fly doesn't see it. It sees the outside through *its* window and keeps head-butting the same window. It has no concept of objective analysis. It does not understand that in order to find its way out, it must initially fly *away* from what appears to be the outside in order to see the window that is open. Of course not – it's a fly! So why do *we* do it then – make the same mistake over and over again?

We follow the crowd. That's why successful parents mostly bring up successful children and welfare parents mostly produce welfare children and it's all to do with following the crowd we're with. If you are not where you want to be in life, you *must* decide to go the other way. Take the road less traveled; be the one lemming going the other way.

The trouble with being the one lemming going the other way is that you have to push your way through all the lemmings coming towards you. Not only that, but every lemming you meet will say, "Hey, dude, stay cool, this is the way, not that way, you got it all wrong." And when you've tried to explain your way past 10^{89} hippy lemmings you become very tired, and very doubtful that you're right and all the others are wrong, and finally you turn and follow the crowd yet again. It's tough to be different.

In order to get what you want, you are going to have to change the way you've tried to get things in the past. That's common sense. Whatever life-plan you have tried this far has, at best, only partially worked, and at worst, hasn't worked at all. This has nothing to do with courage or hard work. You can be, and probably have been, a shining example of courage and work. That isn't the issue. The issue is that your courage and energy have been focused on going bud-doiing against the window. We need to refocus. We need to think.

Arguably the one thing that separates man from the wee beasties is our ability to think. Paradoxically, as Earl Nightingale says in *Leading the Field*, the one thing people try to avoid at all costs is thinking. So millions are spent each week on trying to win a lottery in which the odds of winning are the same as being murdered seven times. But buying a ticket requires no thought.

Isn't it strange? Isn't it a uniquely excellent irony, worthy of the Devil himself, that the one creation on this planet that has been given an infinite capacity for thought, a godlike link with creation that allows him to rethink and recreate his own version of that creation, has absolutely no desire to use it? Indeed he will go out of his way – spend money, get others to think for him, hand over his life and cash to people he's never heard of – just to avoid using this unique gift from God.

Your first step to achieving everything you ever wanted in life is a simple one. Stop relying on other people's thinking as a replacement for your own. Keep your own counsel. Seek second opinions. Don't do what people say without looking closely at what those same people *do*. Success has nothing to do with luck, education, or being in the right place at the right time. Nor has it to do with careers, home businesses, or off-the-shelf business opportunities. It's all to do with understanding who you are and what you want. It's all to do with understanding the powers you have and having the confidence to wield them. It's all to do with getting out of your own way.

Success engineering

The science of success engineering is simply the knowledge of how things work. It is also the simple acceptance that the bridges you have built so far have not worked too well, and the answer is not to do the same things – build the same bridges – over and over again. The answer is to look at where you want to be, not where you are now, and simply decide to get there. If your life-plan hasn't worked, then it's not you that's at fault, it's the plan. Change the plan.

The power to completely and utterly change your entire life is already within you. Indeed, you are where you are today because of that same power – you just didn't know how to harness it. It's not even as if people make "wrong" decisions. In most cases people don't make decisions at all. In these circumstances it's surprising that life is as good as it is. You can correct a wrong decision, but how can you correct a perpetual fence-sitter who doesn't even know why they're on the fence?

Success engineering has natural rules, rules that are crafted from a mix of psychology, business studies, and now, physics. Understand these things, and your life will change:

1. You will *never* get what you want until you know *exactly* what it is you want. You cannot get a flight to "warm and sunny" even though most flights go there. Decide the life you want first – the things, the house, the sort of day you'd like to live – *first*. Which flights to take to these personal destinations only become clear *after* you have chosen the destinations.

2. Do not confuse the flight with the destination. Money is not an end. It is the *means* to an end. Jobs, businesses, and careers are not an end for most people; they are what they think they need to do in order to achieve a certain lifestyle. If the lifestyle turns out wrong, as it does in most cases, it's because they never decided on the lifestyle they wanted in the first place.

3. Goal-setting is absolutely essential. If you cannot, at any time in the future, recite your number one goal immediately, then you're not serious and your life will reflect it.

4. The great problem is inner self-belief. You *must* have one goal for self-belief. Ideally you should have three goals: for self-belief, confidence, and perseverance.

5. Goals must be read and visualized at least twice a day. Imagine if your number one goal came true two hours ago. How would you feel? You'd feel great! (If you didn't, it's hardly a goal, is it?) Now capture that feeling. Hold it at least twice a day.

6. Goal-setting – success engineering – is not a project management exercise. It's either ancient magic, spiritual philosophy, or quantum physics. At the end of the day it matters not one jot whether you engineer your future by drawing circumstances to you like a magnet, "resonating with the power of the celestial sphere," or performing a trans-dimensional quantum leap. So long as it works, who cares?

7. A correctly managed goal may materialize the object of your goal out of thin air but is more likely to produce a workable plan for its achievement. Once you have a plan, it becomes a project management exercise in which you can add dates and targets and break the whole thing down into manageable steps. Either way you must *do* something, *you must take action.* Your goal will come towards you at the same speed you walk towards it. Usually faster. Remember that just imagining your true soul mate probably won't have him/her walk up to your front door and ask if you're in. Get out and mix!

8. You do not live in the ordered world you think you do. This world works by having multiple versions of reality, and which version you live in is determined solely and exclusively by the decisions you make every day. Success engineering is nothing more than making a series of firm decisions. Those decisions load the dice in favor of that outcome.

9. If you read the great religious and spiritual works of old and look at the writings of those enlightened people who speak of such things today, you will see that never in the course of modern history has science been so close to spirituality. Of all branches of science, none are closer to this than quantum mechanics. Miracles and magic are about to become science.

10. Decide exactly what you want. Make goals for them. Simply decide, without hesitation, deviation, or procrastination but with confidence that you will, absolutely, attain these things, and they will happen. Now go and fluff up a few clouds.

* * *

Go forward boldly and unseen forces will come
to your aid.

– Earl Nightingale

* * *

Chapter Eleven
Reality Check

 IN HIS BOOK *Supernature,* Dr Lyall Watson tells the story of one of the first women to be allowed to enter a Tibetan monastery as a trainee. Part of the rigorous training involved being woken at three in the morning in order to meditate. One of the many aspects of training was to create, in your own mind, an imaginary friend. Children do this all the time, but in a monastery it is much more serious, involving many hours of meditation both inside and outside your cell until eventually you have complete command of all the fine details.

Some six months later she was allowed to visit the local market place for a few days. On the final day, one of the villagers asked her who had been accompanying her on previous visits. She said she'd come alone. But the villager said that she had been accompanied by a monk he hadn't seen before and proceeded to describe this new monk in precise detail. It was her "imaginary" monk-friend. Several other villagers confirmed this. When she explained this to her teacher at the monastery, he said that she had successfully completed this aspect of the training and told her to now remove this new friend from her mind.

Having an imaginary friend is fine – until other people start seeing him too, it seems.

You are made up entirely of atoms. You stand on atoms and live among atoms. When you speak, atoms move, and their movement is picked up by other people, who are themselves little more than large clouds of atoms. If you could control the forces between atoms, you could pass though "solid" objects much as a cloud would pass through another cloud. But this cannot happen because then the two clouds would mix together in a very unsavory manner, and we can't have people doing that all the time. You are also in the unique position of being a cloud of atoms that is self-aware and considers its own existence.

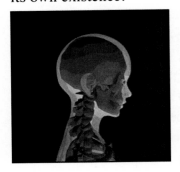

You perceive the world through your eyes. You see things based entirely on visible light, which ranges in wavelength from about 380 nm. to 780 nm. This is why grass looks green and icebergs look bluish-white. But there are lots more wavelengths than these, and if you just select the longer ones and take a look at the same world with infrared, you will see an entirely different world in which grass can be blue and icebergs can be red lumps floating in a green sea. You will see inside people, through their skin. Your beautiful lover can turn into a monster by simply changing a wavelength.

When you touch something, the nerves in your fingers send an electrochemical message to your brain telling you something is there.

If you artificially stimulate those nerves, you will feel something that doesn't exist. Amputees still feel their lost limbs. The reality is that you have no idea whether something is there or not. All you *know* is that your thoughts are working.

You could have been created, fully formed, one minute ago with all your "past" experiences hardwired into you, and you could not prove this to be wrong. It could be that nothing, absolutely nothing, exists beyond the point where your skin meets the air (or what you think is skin – or air). All you see, feel, touch, taste, and hear are just impulses created inside of you, impulses you *think* are outside of you.

You really have no idea of who you are or what you are. You may not exist at all. You may be a thought by someone else. You may be E.T.'s imaginary friend. Or God's.

And if this is true, which it is, then everything outside of you is only real in the sense that you are experiencing a set of powerful feelings that are in harmony with other people's powerful feelings, assuming they exist at all. You cannot prove you're *not* in the Matrix!

All this is true, and seen like this, doesn't the idea of you (or the you you think you are) existing inside different copies of the same plan – different universes – seem more possible?

You are a child of God, a dolphin of the Universe. And if, according to your persuasion, you have been crafted in the image of the Creator, then logically you must be a creator yourself and have some measure of control over that same creation. We are just discovering how much control we have.

Yet pain seems so real, as do worry and fear and hurt and heartbreak, and while these apocalyptic horsemen exist, it is difficult to imagine any kind of different world for ourselves, let alone work towards the ultimate world of our own making.

But love also exists, as do joy and courage and hope and honor. And, however great and complex the vision or reality of our personal Matrix is, I firmly believe that with these guardian angels, and many more like them, we have been given the tools to change things.

From now on, living in hell is voluntary.

It always was.

I wish you all I wish myself.
Thank you for your time.
Phil Gosling

Appendix A

How to Be in Two Places
at the Same Time

A modern experiment at being in two places at the same time and talking to each other while you're doing it! These are real experiments performed in real laboratories with decidedly unreal results.

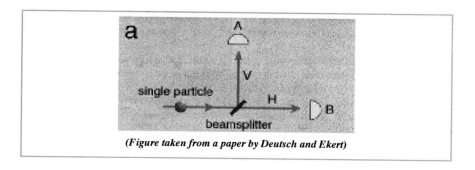

(Figure taken from a paper by Deutsch and Ekert)

Here a light source emits a photon along a path towards a half-silvered mirror (beam splitter). This mirror splits the light, reflecting half vertically toward detector A and transmitting half toward detector B. A photon, however, is a single quantized packet of light and cannot be split, so it is detected with equal probability at either A or B. Intuition would say that the photon randomly leaves the mirror in either the vertical *or* horizontal direction. However, quantum mechanics predicts that the photon actually travels *both* paths simultaneously! *(Figure taken from a paper by Deutsch and Ekert)* This is more clearly demonstrated in figure b. (*Source – Caltech*)

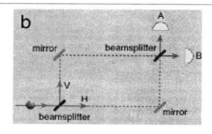

In this experiment, the photon first encounters a half-silvered mirror then a fully silvered mirror, and finally another half-silvered mirror before reaching a detector, where each half-silvered mirror introduces the probability of the photon traveling down one path or the other. Once a photon strikes the mirror along either of the two paths after the first beam splitter, the arrangement is identical to that in figure a, and so one might hypothesize that the photon will reach either detector A or detector B with equal probability. However, experiment shows that in reality this arrangement causes detector A to register 100% of the time, and never at detector B! How can this be?

Figure b depicts an interesting experiment that demonstrates the phenomenon of single-particle interference. In this case, experiment shows that the photon always reaches detector A, never detector B! If a single photon travels vertically and strikes the mirror, then, by comparison to the experiment in figure a, there should be an equal probability that the photon will strike either detector A or detector B. The same goes for a photon traveling down the horizontal path. However, the actual result is drastically different. **The only conceivable conclusion is therefore that the photon somehow traveled both paths simultaneously,** creating an interference at the point of intersection that destroyed the possibility of the signal reaching B. This is known as *quantum interference* and results from the *superposition* of the possible photon *states*, or potential paths. So although only a single photon is emitted, it appears as though an identical photon exists and travels the "path not taken," only detectable by the interference it causes with the original photon when their paths come together again. If, for example, either of the paths are blocked with an absorbing screen, then detector B begins registering hits again just as in the first experiment! This unique characteristic, among others, makes the current research in quantum computing not merely a continuation of today's idea of a computer, but rather an entirely new branch of thought. And it is because quantum computers harness these special characteristics that they have the potential to be incredibly powerful computational devices.

(Source: Caltech, from an original paper used by Neil Gershenfeld in a paper on quantum computing published in *Scientific American*.)

Think of it this way. You walk out of your office at 5:00 p.m. and have the choice of two corridors, left and right, but both will take you to the exit door. Later on in the bar you meet Alice, who saw you walk down the left-hand corridor at 5:01 p.m. because her office happens to be on that corridor. But Bob says he saw you walk by his office, on the right-hand corridor, at 5:01 p.m. because Bob's office is on that corridor. They each think the other is mistaken. You know they're not. Cool, isn't it?

While we're on the physics page I'd like to add a footnote. I've not been concerned that Niels Bohr, one of the fathers of modern physics, and Hugh Everett, the "inventor" of the multi-universe theory, did not see eye to eye, or that Schrödinger invented his cat analogy to have a go at Niels Bohr. I've cross-referenced several ideas, but seeing that no one really knows entirely what's going on, let's call it "the spirit of exploration."

You must be good at one of two things: planting in the spring, or begging in the fall.

– Jim Rohn

Appendix B
The Dating Game – Final Conclusion

A goal, any goal, comes into reality based on *the confident expectation that it will be so*. Some call this the Law of Attraction. My view is that it is the Law of Creation, a probability theory not dissimilar to Appendix A and the first paragraph of Appendix C. *The greater the expectation of an event, the greater the probability dice are loaded in favor of that outcome*.

This law, in whatever form, never stops working. If you have a goal, then every second you spend in the positive expectation of that goal is a second in which the wheels and cogs of the universe realign themselves to create that goal. In the same way, having doubts and fears about that goal doesn't stop the process of creation. Creation still takes place, only this time the concentration is on the doubt; therefore, the opposite outcome is being created. So be careful what you're thinking.

For this reason it is vital to not create doubt and uncertainty. And with that, we can look at the full reasoning regarding *not* putting dates on future goals. It depends on how you're wired.

In Bob Proctor's magnificent series of lectures regarding the power of goal-setting, he refers to the fact that setting a goal is tantamount to sowing a seed. We do not know the gestation period for that seed to spring forth, we just know it will happen at some point in the future. His philosophy is to set a time frame by making an educated guess. If the goal is not visible when that time frame is complete, it simply means that our "best guess" at the gestation period of the goal was a little out, and we merely have to add some extra time.

There is nothing wrong with this argument. The problem may be how you as a person are wired up to deal with it. If you can see that the time period was merely a "best guess" and you can, *without diminution of enthusiasm*, simply carry on by making a new date, then fine, do it that way.

If, on the other hand, you are the type of person who may feel a sense of failure regarding the time element, then don't use a time element.

The important thing is the avoidance of doubt, because doubt, not time, is the final arbiter of whether you will succeed or not.

Whether you believe you can do a thing or not, you are right.

– Henry Ford

Doubt is the great killer of personal success. It creates the opposite universe to the one you wanted. Goal creation is not a straight-line graph. This means that some people get edgy or worried when, at the halfway point, they are clearly no nearer their goal. If you are this kind of person, then setting dates will induce stress. So don't set dates.

Your great subconscious mind, the real you, the 90%+ of your soul that has its own personal Internet connection with creation itself, only sees images and feels feelings. It does not make judgments or logical conclusions. If your image is one of health, wealth, and happiness, and you have feelings of joy and warmth – the feelings of a victor –associated with that vision, then that is all you need to clothe that image in reality. And it will happen with surprising speed.

Appendix C
Quantum Car Parking

The essence of quantum/probability theory is that nothing is real – you only have options or probabilities. Everything you see is there simply because the act of seeing it caused one of several zillion options to materialize into form. Which one of those options appeared is decided either at random, or by what you expected to see.

I'm currently sitting in my room tapping away at the keyboard of a Toshiba SM30-604. About one mile away is the main street of my local village, a street I cannot physically see from here. I know that cars will be parked on each side of the street and that usually the street is pretty full of cars. I obviously have no idea which particular car is in which particular place. Here is where quantum physics devotees and normal, sane people differ.

If I were normal I would assume that the town and street exist in real time and that at this moment real cars are parked in real spaces even though I cannot see them. I believe that when I drive down there I will see a situation which really exists and over which I have no control. Cars are parked in various spaces, and my finding a place to park is merely a matter of luck or persistence. It's a fait accompli.

Quantum lunatics see it this way: The cars and street don't exist in real time. They are figments of my imagination – possibilities, alternatives. Furthermore, there are an infinite number of car/parking combinations available. There is one *possibility* that a parking space outside say, the bank, is occupied by a Ford, and another that it may be a Jaguar. All these possibilities, like Schrödinger's pussycat, are only possibilities *until I set eyes upon the situation*. Like lifting the lid. So let's do just that.

Without goal-setting, all these possibilities are like picking the winner of a lottery out of a hat. I go down to the village, and the winner I picked was a Ford in front of the bank. That's the one scenario that was forced into existence *at random* the moment I set eyes on it. In the same way that opening the lid to the cat experiment always reveals *something* – a live or deceased mouser – one possibility always leaps into existence the moment you look at it.

With goal-setting the situation is different. By concentrating on *one* particular outcome – just one of the many probabilities available – *I load the dice in favor of that outcome*. It's that simple. By *expecting* the scenario with the free space in front of the bank, I tip the random balance of probabilities in favor of that outcome simply by believing that it will take place.

Normal people believe that life *is*, that events *are*, and that they have little control over those events. Physicists believe that nothing is real, that any event is merely one of several zillion options that are available at any time, and that these events become real only when you look at them. Scientific philosophers[6] believe that goal-

---

[6] "Metaphysics" means "beyond the physical." A scientific philosopher takes real science and tries to expand its meaning beyond the laboratory. The two ideas are not the same. But they can be. Like most things, it just depends which way you look at it

setting allows us to use just a little of our 240,000 million, million kilowatt-hours of energy to tip the probability balance in our favor. Theologians, metaphysicians, spiritual thinkers, and students of "the science of success" have known this for a long time. What is happening now is that quite a few serious scientists are opening up to the understanding that what happens at a very small scale may affect us in more ways than many people currently dare to think.

The whole of your life and all the things in it – money, love, health, relationships, cars, houses, vacations, mothers-in-law, good luck and bad luck – are just a series of possibilities that came true largely at random simply because you never realized that you hold the remote control – the clicker – on your own life. You don't need intelligence because there is a whole universal consciousness – the background radiation from millions of people alive and dead who shared some of their 2.4×10^{17} KwH with you – and this is out there for you to plug into.

Everything you cannot physically see with your eyes at this present moment doesn't exist. My wife has just left to collect Timmy from school. She will come back into my life looking as she did when she left because I have the absolute expectation that this will be so.

There is nothing you cannot change, nothing you cannot control, nothing you cannot bring into your personal self-created universe, nothing you cannot *cannot*, because *cannot* and *can't* no longer exist. You have the channel changer of your life in your hands, and every channel button has the word "believe" or "expect" written on it in pleasant, soothing letters.

Now it's in your hands. Just change the channel to the one you want, not the one somebody else chose for you since the day you were born.

Appendix D
Musings of Life and Science

IN 1614, the polymath Galileo Galilei had a little bit of a problem with the established church of the day. Basically, his theory that the earth revolved around the sun ran contrary to the Unholy Roman Inquisition's view of nature, and their notion of informed debate was to threaten to poke his eyes out if he didn't start seeing things their way.

Not only did this affect Galileo, it also had a dramatic, if hidden knock-on effect on every scientist of the day. Consciously or otherwise, the lords of science decided to keep their eyeballs and took 'life' out of science. From that day forth, scientific investigation that dealt with purely physical, repeatable phenomena became even more rigorously physical and devoid of life. Objects were objects. Things happened through cause and effect alone. Anything to do with life, religion, God, or the spiritual realm was left to theologians. Science became atheist. It had little choice.

Of course science, by definition, is there to seek rational solutions to physical phenomena, so the real change was not only an acute concentration on the physical but an active antipathy toward anything that wasn't strictly rational and provable by experimentation.

Ironically the god of objectivity had a hidden, subjective agenda – to disprove all other gods.

Science won a pivotal victory when Darwinism triumphed over Creationism. In a debate that is argued to this day, evolution still rules triumphant in a battle that may have been fought without the instruments of physical torture on the one side, but the other, desperate to gain authority, had a few irrational knuckle-dusters of their own hidden inside the gloves.

This is not about that debate. The point is that history placed the rationalism of science at the opposite end of those who believe that life itself has an influence on scientific phenomena. After nearly 400 years, science in the form of quantum physics suddenly hit a barrier to its life-free zone called 'The Observer'.

In the movies, *"What the bleep to we know"* and *"Down the rabbit hole,"* Dr Fred Alan Wolf Ph.D., aka "Dr Quantum" explains the infamous "double slit experiment". This was the one I mentioned in Chapter 4 regarding what happens when photons are shot through double slits. Let's use electrons instead of photons.

Single electrons (which are 'stuff' – physical matter) shot through two slits produced unexpected wave patterns on the other side. Like photons, we know now this is to do with the same particle going in two (in fact, multiple) directions at the same time. But here's the real enigma. If you place a measuring device to see what's going on in the system – then this device – the "observer" – affects the outcome, and the electron pattern goes back to the two lines of particles. It's important to remember that the measuring device or observer in no way physically affected the experiment. It wasn't as if the timekeeper in the 100m Olympic sprint had stood in the middle of the track. He was off the track, just measuring and observing. Yet what happens is that this timekeeper still affects the outcome of the race *as if* he was part of the race itself. In the words of Dr Wolf, "It's as if the electron decided to act differently; *as though it was aware it was being watched* ... the observer collapsed the wave function, simply by observing." This of course is completely irrational, illogical and cannot happen in physics or anything else. Every physical effect has a physical cause. And yet it happens. Looking at an event changes the outcome of the event. Consciousness – the state of being alive – affects the outcome of an event. The physicists who argue this point grow fewer each day. The only argument is why does it do so, and by how much.

In this one simple experiment, 400 years of scientific dogma unravels like a ball of superstrings. 'Consciousness' (i.e., life) is woven into the fabric of all things. It is made visible only at the tiniest level, in a place where mathematics proves everything, and trying to turn what the math tells us into some form of picture has gone beyond all but the most artistic of physicists. Physics, the science that was created to replace pure thought with experimentation and still seeks to reduce everything, including life, to a single equation, has unwittingly become the first to acknowledge the existence of life within the fabric of matter.

The questions today are, is energy intelligent? If so, are we part of that intelligence? Can we control it?

My answer is yes.

In 1910, Wallace D. Wattles wrote *The Science of Getting Rich*, a seminal work which has become one of the cornerstones of modern success thinking. In this book he wrote:

The stuff from which all things are made is a substance which thinks,
and a thought of form in this substance produces the form.

Today, if I had to paraphrase that sentence I would write:

The energy from which everything is made, and flows through
all things and the spaces in between, is an intelligent energy that
responds to thought and observation. It responds to life, and life has
the capacity to influence it.

Is that intelligence God?

That, my friend, is several steps beyond where even I am prepared
to go.

* * *

Consciousness is the ground of all being,
matter, including the brain ...
When we observe matter, we choose from among (many)
possibilities to produce the actual event that we experience.

– Dr Amit Goswami, Emeritus professor
of physics. University of Oregon

* * *

The Unified Field, according to modern physics, is the deepest, most powerful level of Nature's functioning – and the source of the infinite creativity and intelligence within every individual and displayed throughout the universe.

– Dr John Hagelin Ph.D.

* * *

I feel like we're on the verge of a gigantic discovery – maybe the nature of God, maybe the nature of the human spirit. Something of that sort is going to emerge from this, because our normal notions – in fact the notions upon which we think science makes any sense at all, the notions of space and time and matter – they just are breaking down, they're just falling apart, like tissue paper before our eyes .

– Prof. Fred Alan Wolf Ph.D.

* * *

Dare to think.

– Phil Gosling

Notes

Notes

Notes

Lightning Source UK Ltd.
Milton Keynes UK

177872UK00001BA/167/P